BADER FIELD

A Journey of Love, Forgiveness and Acceptance

Carl David

©2008
Nightengale Press
A Nightengale Media LLC Company

For information about Nightengale Press please
visit our website at www.nightengalepress.com.
Email: publisher@nightengalepress.biz
or send a letter to:
Nightengale Press
10936 N. Port Washington Road. Suite 206
Mequon, WI 53092
Library of Congress Cataloging-in-Publication Data

David, Carl,
BADER FIELD/ Carl David
ISBN:1-933449-66-7
ISBN 13: 978-1933449-66-1
Biogrpahy

Copyright Registered: 2008
First Published by Nightengale Press in the USA

December 2008

10 9 8 7 6 5 4 3 2 1

Printed in the USA and the UK

Dedication

I dedicate this book to you, Pop, as a memorial to your love. I miss you...I believe you know.

To Mom, the splendid other half of his greatness. With unfaltering love always.

To Alan, never forget his love for you.

To Bruce, you will live in our hearts forever. I miss you....

For Arlyn, I'm grateful for the time you knew and loved him; I regret the brevity. He loved you as his daughter. I love you for all of the richness in love you have given to me. We are forever!

For our sons, Shawn and Brett, you must endure the worst loss in never having known Pop. A lifetime of apologies couldn't forgive that, but perhaps through all of us and through our love you'll feel his soul and his deep love for you. So much of him lives within you both.

Acknowledgements

Special thanks to Mom for her endless love and support and for always being there for all of us, unconditionally.

Special thanks to Arlyn, my precious wife and soul mate, for everything, but most of all for your magnificent love; you are a gift. I am so blessed. I love you!

Special thanks to Shawn and Brett, our loving children of whom we are so very proud. We are so blessed to have you as our sons and friends. You are great people. We love you dearly!

Special thanks to Alan, you have always been a great brother and our closeness will stay solid, no matter the geographical distance. I couldn't have done it without you.

Special thanks to Jaki Baskow of Baskow & Associates, for believing in me and this book and for leading me to Nightengale Press, but most of all for being a dear friend.

Special thanks to Valerie Connelly of Nightengale Press for her vision and faith in my book. She "got it." I am very grateful to be a member of the Nightengale Press family! You are the best!

Special thanks to my editor, Yvonne Perry of Writers in the Sky Creative Writing Services. You are a genius! I am so very fortunate to have been able to work with you to make this book come to life.

Special thanks to Bob Ruffalo of Princeton Books for some of the photographs of the Shelburne Hotel in Atlantic City.

Special thanks to you, Pop, for being my father. You gave me a lifetime of love and richness in too few years. I live on with you in my heart and soul always.

Introduction

Sam David was one of the greatest art dealers of all time. Respected, revered, and feared for his knowledge of the art business. He possessed an uncanny ability to determine the next trend in art before it was conceived, and be there to stake his claim as it unfolded. He was anything but a traditionalist. Things were done "Sammy's way" or not at all. He ran his business like a tight ship. There was no nonsense, and nothing could deter his will to make his mark in the art world.

I watched him from the time I was a kid with never an opportunity wasted. If there was a chance to put a deal together, Sam would be there. More times than not, he'd hop into his airplane and get to places commercial airlines wouldn't dream of landing. At times, it was difficult to understand what lured him to the fiery success he achieved, but this was a driven man with a raw passion for life. Consumed by the everlasting search for the treasure, he struck oil on more occasions than could be counted. He recognized quality with a cunning instinct, and could separate good, better, and best in an instant.

Born and raised in New York, he was dealing Old Master paintings from the time he was fifteen years old. He was dazzled by the extraordinary skills of these thirteenth to seventeenth century masters who could create timeless images with military precision. He'd study their examples at the Metropolitan Museum and wherever else he could view them.

His father, David David, moved the family to Philadelphia where they established the next of several antiquarian galleries. By 1960, Sam David had purchased a great building half a block south of Rittenhouse Square that still houses the David David Art Gallery. The main course being a combination of Old Master, French Impressionism, American Impressionism, American landscape, and American primitive paintings, as well as all of the decorative arts associated with them.

David David Gallery

Until his untimely death in 1973, Sam had discovered and either purchased or managed exclusively, the estates of at least four major Philadelphia artists with international reputations. He saved a world class mural from the Shelburne Hotel in Atlantic City days before it was to be razed, and promoted scores of museum exhibitions, in which his own inventories were players. There were countless victories and certain losses as well.

His art and his flying were his vices in life, but above all else, his family was of paramount importance to him. No better father could anyone even imagine. He was always giving to others, and he earned their love and respect in return. However, the loss of a son etched a nightmare in his mind, which eventually robbed him of life, and placed the family art business squarely on the shoulders of his sons, Alan and me—Carl, the author of this book.

Sam's quest for excellence has been preserved as the fourth generation of the firm carries on in precisely the same manner of intensity, with unwavering integrity and dedication equal to Sam's. Today, I carry on the family business with my wife Arlyn, and our sons Shawn and Brett, who have inherited the same love and passion of a great man, Sam David.

foreword

When I first started the developmental and copy edit for this book, I knew I held a jewel in my hands. I had come upon a skilled writer with a superb story of movie-like quality. It has the drama of human emotion stirred by true events that bring lovable characters to life. Plus, there are interesting historical facts intertwined throughout the telling. Add some mysterious and ghostly happenings to those components and you have a great book—*Bader Field*.

I was not familiar with the art world that is common and everyday life for the David family, but I learned things in this book that caused me to better appreciate all art forms around me—even the art of life itself. I also learned quite a bit about flying twin-engine airplanes, which is a huge love the author shared with his dad. The book is named after the airfield that launched Carl and his dad to the skies where they enjoyed hundreds of flight hours reveling in their distinctive father-son bond.

Even though the book follows a chronological time line, each chapter has an embedded memory or flashback that lands us in the middle of an exciting, tragic, or educational event. Whether a childhood winter moment as the David boys take their dad for the sled ride of his life; or the account of how a famous piece of art was acquired; or the bygone days of the Depression Era when Sam and Flora first met—this book details a heartfelt journey that demonstrates the healing that comes from letting go of the past and living only for what is before us in this moment.

Carl has a great knack for storytelling and a gift for showing us what is in his heart. *Bader Field* allows a reader to see the inside impact that the self-inflicted death of a loved one has on an entire family and how much spiritual strength it takes to move past such devastation.

We may never meet the David family in person, but after reading *Bader Field*, I promise you will feel as if you have known them all your life. You may even feel like part of the family and be tempted to refer to Sam David as "Pop." He might even visit you in spirit!

Yvonne Perry, Editor
Author of *More Than Meets the Eye, True Stories about Death, Dying, and Afterlife* and *Right to Recover, Winning the Political and Religious Wars over Stem Cell Research in America*

BADER FIELD

A Journey of Love, Forgiveness and Acceptance

Chapter One

The End

The telephone rang at 3:50 a.m. ripping me from a fitful sleep and slamming me back into my body. I lunged for the phone on the nightstand through the early morning blackness.

"It's all over...," my mother's voice faltered. "Your father's dead!" I felt as though my guts had suddenly been wrenched from my body.

"What?" *It's not possible.* "We were just with him a few days ago in Atlantic City; he was fine." I suddenly felt sick to my stomach.

"He wasn't feeling well before he left for London, promised me he'd see a heart man when he got back." Mom was crying.

"Oh, My God!" As I sat up shaking, I dug my hands into the sheets and shivered, hoping this was just a bad dream. My wife, Arlyn, sat up next to me. "Oh, my God, Mom. W-w-what happened?"

"Your father was on his way upstairs to get dressed after having his morning coffee. Julius heard him yell for help, ran to him as he collapsed on the stairs, clutching his chest."

"Are you home?"

"He was dead instantly, son. It all happened so fast. There wasn't anything we could do. It just happened so fast!"

"Mom? Arlyn and I will be right there."

"I have nothing to live for..... my life is over."

Click.

"Mom? MOM!"

Life as I had known it would never be the same after that call in 1973. How I wished that telephone call had been in error.

Julius had telephoned my mother from London when it happened. It was the hardest call he had ever had to make. Sammy had been his best friend and now he was gone. All he could offer Flora was, "You let me know if there is anything at all I can do for you and your family. I will be here for you." It seemed so inadequate for consoling a new widow.

Julius had looked upon Pop as the son he never had, and whenever Pop was in London on business he stayed at Julius' house at 10 Farm Street. They would spend days and nights together, living the art world until they dropped from exhaustion. The only respite was television, which Julius absolutely adored. Their cricket matches were one of two interruptions that were compellingly scheduled. The other was gourmet lunch and dinner during which they continued their art business dialogue, the essential ingredient which fueled the fire of these two experienced dealers. Julius loved "Sammy" as he affectionately referred to him. He was intrigued by his affable nature and his love of paintings; especially the Old Masters which was Julius' personal specialty. They got on well together, sharing various trade secrets and gossip, which were never heard outside of that house. They were in awe of one another's encyclopedic knowledge, which they spouted proudly to impress themselves. Their relationship required perpetual stamina to maintain. It was woven with work, work, and more work, and held together by a rigid fiber of friendship which lasted to the bitter end.

I sat on the side of the bed in a state of twilight, fraught with the unreality of Pop's death as Arlyn tried to comfort me. My life's teacher was destroyed with one quick gesture of mortality. Perhaps, even in death his final lesson to me was demonstrating that time on Earth is only borrowed—temporary at best. Pop was a vibrant fifty-eight years of age and though I always knew that he would burn out early, the premature nature of his death was criminal. This was one trauma I would never let time erase.

I didn't know what to say. I was stunned and feeling numb from the whole thing. I just couldn't believe it had happened. I called my eldest brother, Alan. Mom had already told him.

"Are you okay?" Alan was the strong one of the family.

"I'm all right," I lied. I was scared to death.

"I'm leaving New York immediately. I'll meet you at Mom's in about an hour and a half.

Arlyn and I jumped into our jeans and headed for the apartment located in a prestigious area of Philadelphia a block south of Rittenhouse Square. The morning's light was dawning as we drove through transient space. I was crazed with a mixture of fear, anger, and grief. I ran red lights, and raced relentlessly to my remaining parent. I no longer gave a damn about rules or anything else mortal. None of it made sense anymore. How could anyone compare the sudden loss of my father to anything earthly?

We made the normal thirty-minute trip from the northeast to Center City in about twelve minutes in my 1967 Cutlass Supreme. The sun was peeking above the horizon as we parked the car in front of the gallery adjacent to the new apartment house Mom and Pop had shared until two hours before. The doormen greeted us with their condolences to which we nodded gratefully. The elevator ride was brief but seemed to take forever. We walked into Mom's apartment. She looked ghastly. I went over to her and put my arms around her and held her close.

"I can't believe it; my life is over!" Mom sobbed her newfound mantra over and over. I was worried about losing her, too. She and Pop were as close as any man and woman could ever be. They were more than married; they were intimate on all levels, frequently able to communicate without a spoken word. They knew each other's minds, wants, likes, and dislikes. They were the epitome of spiritual blending, a unit unto themselves able to exist under any circumstances. They grew closer with each passing day and they thrived on the excitement of new experiences. Nothing could ever deter them from one another because they lived in love. It was extraordinary to grow up under such a benevolent sparkling shower of affection, for no matter what failed, there was always the comfort and reassuring love of my parents upon which I could depend. It took the awesome and relentlessly destructive force of death to sever their bond. Death, which could limit future activity, was powerless to eliminate history. My memories would continue to provide me with the solace and inspiration to persevere.

Mom would need us now more than ever; but we also needed her to survive this horrible ordeal. She had been through an awful lot as a child, so hardships of life were no stranger to this indomitable lady. Both of her parents had died senselessly when she was still quite young. Her father, at age forty five, had caught double pneumonia at the funeral of her grandmother, and subsequently died thereafter. There was no cure for an ailment like that in those days. The flu or a bad cold made chances for survival dim because of attendant complications and developments. Antibiotics were a glint of the future, then nonexistent, so old home remedies were the prime modality of medicine. Her mother took ill not long after the passing of her father and eventually died in her early sixties of heart failure.

Mom, and her two sisters, Annabelle and Eve, and three brothers, Arthur, Harold, and Isador were left by themselves to hold together the fragile pieces of their lives. The very eldest was merely a teenager who was thrust out with the adult work force to bring home money to feed and clothe the lot of them.

They had been raised to that point in Erie, Pennsylvania, but decided on a move to Philadelphia where there were some distant relations already established. This decision was made after watching their father's brother run the lucrative family soda bottling plant into the ground. They couldn't cope with any more disaster and felt they would all benefit with a fresh start in the big city far away from their life of recent tragedies.

Mom was the baby sister. She and her brothers and sisters were alone to survive the only way they knew; with love and hard work. Those who were old enough worked full time or after school and on weekends, while the others would take shifts caring for their younger siblings at home. Whatever money they earned was used to provide for each other. In time, they managed to save enough to move into a pretty nice house in a section of Philadelphia called Logan. Theirs was the most popular gathering spot in the neighborhood. All the kids in the area would flock to it to bathe in the newfound pools of love, respect, laughter, and closeness. This was one special clan, who had pulled themselves through very difficult times. They made it, grew up, and all eventually married and had children of their own, never losing their closeness for one another.

"Life's purpose has abandoned me. I don't want to live anymore." Mom sat sobbing uncontrollably.

"Mom, you can't mean that." Arlyn took her hand in hers and held it. "You have a beautiful house and a loving family. We are all here for you."

"Life has no meaning without Sam. What do I need with a place like this?" The grand multi-room apartment, which they had just rented six months before, overlooked Rittenhouse Square on the north side, 18th Street to the east, and you could see almost to the Philadelphia International Airport off to the south. Each view offered either tranquility or excitement. Aside from the beauty of the place, the convenience of being right next to the family-owned gallery would have saved Pop half his life in commuting time alone. It was especially nice to walk a few steps to get home after a grueling day at the office. Besides, that way he could sleep a little bit longer in the morning, or saunter over at ten 'o clock in the evening after dinner if he so desired. "Living here without Sam would only be an empty and lonely experience," Mom cried.

"We are all upset. All of us have lost Pop." I tried to console her, but my own tears were pushing forward with the emotional current. "He wouldn't want you to give up. He would want you to continue to enjoy life. Surely...."

"I cannot endure this, Carl!"

Pop had been utterly comfortable in the many well-proportioned rooms whether it was the library, the living room, the dining room, the kitchen, or either of the bedrooms.

"I'll make a cup of hot tea for you," I said as I headed toward the kitchen to recompose myself.

"I don't want any tea. I don't want to live anymore," Mom continued to wail.

As I walked into the kitchen, I noticed a hand-written message that my father never intended for the rest of the world. It was boldly placed on a message board tacked on the wall by the telephone. It read, "Flora's God is Sam." To the outsider, the interpretation would be one of glaring chauvinism, but to those who knew him, it spoke differently. It was a proud commentary, which boasted of their mutual adoration. I cried when I saw the note. Though it would still retain its meaning, likely for a long time, there was a side of it that only reinforced Pop's terminal absence. It was a statement which couldn't be unified by his presence, and like anything else it was inevitable that the sands of time would watch it fade into memory.

We were all in a state of flux and knew that the world wouldn't wait for us. We had to get our acts together and begin the very slow and persistently painful process of recovery. The first step to be taken was the reclamation of Pop's body. Julius had informed us that even with breaking the English red tape it could easily take from ten days to two weeks to return his body to the States. There was no way in hell we were going to wait such an obscene length of time to retrieve him from overseas. We made it very plain that we wanted him back immediately, and begged Julius to pull any and all strings necessary to expedite matters, and through his political connections and powerful friends he did just that. In just two days, Pop's body arrived at the Philadelphia airport and the funeral was set for the following day. Someone had to go to the airport to meet his body, so Alan was elected. Of course, I had the option to accompany him on the trip but I was absolutely petrified by the idea of seeing Pop dead. I had no notion as to whether or not the body would have to be identified, but I imagined the worst and my stomach quivered with panic at the very thought. I just couldn't bring myself to do it. Alan also went to pick out the casket. I was embarrassed that I didn't have the spine to do these things, but I felt paralyzed. Anyhow, Alan was nine years older than me, and more grown up about such things.

I had been lucky enough to have Pop for twenty-four miraculous years of my life. Some people never have that; others have it and treat it with disregard, and others have fathers who simply inherit the title without earning it. Every child grows up trying to express his innermost feelings of independence, and most parents suppress them by injecting their own philosophies without permitting them to stumble and find their own way, but my father was different. He issued the option of choice, exerting influence only in situations of danger, stupidity, or futility. He insisted only upon respect, obedience, and good manners, for those disciplines were fundamental to success and happiness along the road to independence. I was surely going to miss him, for there are too few people in whom I could place total trust, love, and belief.

I'd had the best father, and though he's been relegated to the past, I still have the memories to cherish and keep alive forever. The painful truth is that memories are just not the same as the real thing, and as a replacement, they are hardly perfect. They are wonderful bits of sentimentality, which thrust you into a pool of nostalgia that gets deeper as you wade farther into the recesses of yesteryear. What's the use? Memories only drag you back to the past, making it more difficult to forget the aching loss by teasing you with wisps of what used to be, while awakening you to the cold and heartless beckoning vacuum.

Everything was settling into a lengthening state of shock. Reality and unreality merged swiftly, and would take years to distinguish again. They had become married in an unhealthy defense, and it would be a well-fought battle, which would undermine their association. My God had been demolished in an instant, never to be again. I was on my own to use the wisdom he had been administering to me patiently in our splendor-filled years together. I vowed to make him proud; I would never again be lazy, or take lightly his commandments, which he never forced upon me, only insisting that I hear, understand, and observe if I deemed it appropriate. He was a visionary and it always mystified me to discover how right he was about things, which I could scarcely even envision. His perception of human behaviors was awesome. He came to be my hero.

BADER FIELD

As I stood in the kitchen that day, I felt my soul agonizing for any children I might have because they would never know their grandfather, except through me and the lessons I would transfer to them. I made a commitment then and there to etch into their young minds every single shred of goodness and wisdom I could furnish, and paint them an everlasting mental portrait of the man. It became my obligation in life to share with them those very extraordinary qualities that I enjoyed so briefly, but so thoroughly, and so permanently. It would be my mission to give them the same enlightenment and engaging energy, which he so willingly donated to me every day of my existence with him.

Fate had made a serious mistake to take him away from me. I would journey through the rest of my life with the sole remembrance that I must take advantage of every single minute while it exists. It won't last forever, and once it's gone it cannot be regained. I had learned the hardest way through death's personal pronouncement. I would never forget the era of pain into which I was about to enter.

Chapter Two

Unfulfilled Promise

Pop had been experiencing some fairly predictable warning signs toward the end. He was feeling more than just vague pressure in his chest every so often. It occurred mostly at night, but it was significant enough that he decided not to waste any time and got himself to the family physician for a physical examination. In the early 1970s, that meant a superficial blood pressure test in conjunction with a urinalysis, cardiogram, and basic blood work. He had undergone a mandatory complete physical for his pilot's license renewal prior to his death. He had passed with flying colors, but his symptoms were persistent enough to cause him sufficient doubt about the medical clearance he had received. A second physical revealed no more than the first. His cardiogram was normal, and his blood pressure was right on target. All signs pointed to a perfectly healthy specimen who either had habitual indigestion or a deep-rooted problem elusive enough to escape detection. Back then, we didn't have an introspective battery of tests like we have today. He questioned why he had difficulty catching his breath after a flight of stairs or during only one block of spirited walking.

He was petrified—not of dying—but of losing his license to fly. If he were to be grounded by the FAA for health reasons, it would have been equal to imprisonment and a punishment he wouldn't have been able to bear. Banishment from the heavens could not be tolerated. And yet, he knew something was amiss in the medical analysis of his body's communication to him. The doctors were telling him that he was fine but he didn't feel it or believe it. He was extraordinary in his perception of things both inward and outward and he just wasn't buying the news from the world of medicine.

Early one morning, he was in the gallery with Annabelle, one of Mom's sisters who worked with us for years, when he confided to her, "Annie, I think I've got a bad ticker." She suggested that he make an appointment with a heart specialist.

How frightening it must have been to count the days, not knowing which would be his last. There was so much to do yet, so much to see, and so little time in which to do it all. He had certainly crammed a lot of life into his brief but fiery years, but it wasn't enough. It's hard to judge who would be more cheated, he who would vanish forever, or everyone he touched who would have to continue on with life's journey without him. It would be a terrible tug of war but there would be no winners.

Alan was also aware of Pop's degenerating strength. He would have to wait while Pop rested for a minute or two, every couple of blocks. How pathetic it must have been to watch helplessly as the irrepressible force of his strength dwindled so rapidly. A few weeks prior to his trip to London, Pop asked Alan, "What would you do if I died tomorrow?" Alan was stunned and totally unable to respond. Filled with worry, he began to contemplate the gelling realism of what he had suspected from the recent weeks of Pop's visibly declining health. Pop knew that Alan would be able to carry on the business, but he wasn't sure of the emotional repercussions of his death. Alan was extremely independent in his ways. At times he felt put upon or restrained from doing his own thing, which caused an occasional tense moment between the two of them. Pop only wanted the best for him, and as parents will do, exerted his opinions when he thought it necessary. Pop needed Alan in the business; he was a hard worker and there was an enormous amount of work to be done. It was nearly impossible as a one-man show, but through the earlier years when Alan was fresh out of Wharton School at the University of Pennsylvania it was pretty much a solo enterprise. Alan wanted to be a stockbroker so he moved to New York and played that hand until he tired of it. He could have done any number of things, but he eventually came back to the family business. As with any two generations, there were differences in opinions and philosophies regarding the most profitable way to administer the business, but for the most part they agreed in principle and worked well together.

Pop's dream was for Alan and me to run the business while he and Mom traveled aimlessly throughout the world, visiting far away lands and traversing foreign bodies of water on luxurious yachts while bathing in the various facets of opulence the world had to offer. Pop was angry at the thought of being cut down in his prime and being robbed of the opportunity to relax a bit in the pleasure-laden years ahead.

In the final few weeks when Pop wasn't feeling well, Arlyn and I would visit with him. In response to our questions of concern he would say, "Aw, it's just indigestion; I'll be okay. Don't worry!" But I wasn't so sure. The antacids weren't working anymore and he wasn't getting any better. The tightening in his chest was becoming too frequent to be coincidental. He still enthusiastically insisted that the four of us go out to dinner at La Panetiere, the best French restaurant in Philadelphia, but we calmed him down and told him that we didn't come to eat, we just came to spend some time with him. It was plain to see that he was suffering discomfort every now and again and when he sat around listlessly, I worried. Though I was seriously concerned about him, it didn't occur to me that he was really mortal. I could not envision his being anything but alive; death was wholly out of the picture.

Could the crushing blow have been averted? The certificate of death indicated that his heart had suffered nearly total calcification, so even a bypass operation might have proven ineffective. In those days, that kind of procedure was relatively avant-garde. Double, triple, and quadruple bypass surgery was nearly unknown then, though if Pop had been afforded the opportunity to be the pioneer experimental patient, he would have unquestionably gone for it. He was not the kind to give up without a fight. One of his poker playing directives was that if you're going to lose it all anyway, throw in everything you've got for the grand finale, and just maybe you'll come out a winner.

The irony in all of this lay in a very private and tender conversation Pop had with Mom the night before he left for London. She made him promise her that he would see a heart specialist as soon as he returned the following week. He swore faithfully to her that he would. That was the only promise he had ever made that he couldn't fulfill.

Chapter Three

The Farewell

A few days before my dad died, I had an uncomfortable feeling that continued to grow silently. Arlyn and I received a surprise phone call early that morning. My parents were flying down to see a client and wanted to know if we could meet them at noon at Bader Field, the Atlantic City airport. My eyes lighted with joy and my response was an eager, "Look for us; Arlyn and I will be waiting for you."

Bader Field was named in honor of a deceased mayor of Atlantic City. One of the oldest airfields in America, it was perched about one-half mile west of the boardwalk so commuters and visitors could easily disembark from single- and twin-engine airplanes and walk into the pulse of the historic seaside resort.

Our game plan was for a brief visit to the client followed by lunch and then we'd take my parents back to Bader Field so they could get back by late afternoon. The thought of spending those few random hours sounded very inviting for some odd reason. It was always fun to be with my folks but this meeting seemed to hold more importance to me. I didn't know why and didn't question it.

Arlyn and I had a quick breakfast and got dressed for a typical Sunday at the shore. We took a quick walk on the boardwalk to quench our senses with the pungent aroma of the salt-laden atmosphere which was mingling with the soft, wafting warm breezes coming off the beach. We looked at one another and smiled in anticipation of the coming hours.

Without hesitation, we bounded together toward the ocean as a barefooted ensemble and splashed in the surf as we held hands. The water was pleasantly tepid as the foaming lather splashed over our ankles. Though time seemed to have lost its direction, the hour was growing late so we headed back to the car, brushed off the layers of sand and aimed for the airport.

It was only a five-minute ride and it was right on the main highway that brought the traffic into Atlantic City. Barely across the causeway, over the canal and we were there. Not a very impressive airport—only a few private hangars, a cement landing strip, a small snack bar building which housed the ground control facility and bathrooms, and a couple of rows of chocked aircrafts to the left and right sides. The absence of the sea breezes was quite noticeable as we were beginning to sweat from the midday sun. As I peered into the distance toward the west, there appeared a glittering shimmer which had to be them. In another minute or so, that incredibly beautiful red and white twin-engine bird that I knew so well would be touching down. I stared into space and watched her grow larger by the second as it closed the distance between us. Suddenly, she was fully recognizable. The wing and belly strobes were flashing discordantly, but rhythmically. They were just over the threshold with a nose up attitude and gear down. They seemed to just float to the ground. A slight screech as the tires kissed the runway, and they were here.

The Aztec made a sweet symphonic sound as she approached. It was a harmonious purr exuding the metallic smell of power. The strobes turned off and the engines leaned out to a sputtering halt ending in silence. The latch on the door released and the door opened as we ran up to them in an exchange of warm embraces. Suddenly, life was an encrusted jewel glittering with every turn of its facets. There was an outpouring of blue-white light warming everyone in its path as it created an almost euphoric energy. I didn't just hold Pop; I clutched him and wished this moment never to finish. There was an immediate bond that stretched beyond our embrace throughout the afternoon. I hadn't seen Pop for several days since he'd been to Chicago to close on some serious negotiations involving some very rare and important nineteenth-century paintings. It had been a smashing success.

Pop was beaming about the Winslow Homer and the Thomas Eakins as he retold his story. It was a certainty that when he set out on a mission he would return the victor.

"It was a real coup! It was a tough deal, but I managed to outwit the competition and throw them off balance by feigning disinterest in the real meat of the deal," he explained. "The other dealers would discreetly follow me around and watch closely if I showed interest in something. If I passed over it without so much as a glance they would assume something was wrong with it." It thrilled me to watch him devour his competition who would have stabbed him in the back if given the chance. "If it were a treasure, they surmised, Sam David would be after it like a herd of elephants."

I had watched with admiration all my life as he so skillfully performed with deadly accuracy. Pop knew how to deal and when to overpay, for when the potential was there, the excess tens of thousands of dollars invested in the front end of the deal were inconsequential.

BADER FIELD

Pop was the most positive thinking and acting super achiever I'd ever known. He was a stunning force of one; a dynamo of individual power. He never set the guns down. Not for a minute! He was a master of situation alteration. If something didn't suit him, or failed to meet with his approval, he would tailor it until it conformed to his design. He was never tolerant of the tail wagging the dog as it were, and reminded me of that more than once. I was still a bit green around the edges, slightly cocky, and more than a touch skeptical of this seemingly overpowering style, but as time passed, his methods grew on me even though his manner didn't seem quite my size yet. I marveled at his grace and immense wealth of knowledge about human behavior, but I wasn't feeling the sufficient degree of adequacy to assume the role just yet. After all, how could anyone match such a perpetual show of strength? The one thing I would never do would be to hurt him. I would have focused the pain in any other direction, even inward. At the naive age of twenty-four, the thought of practicing his ideology was tantamount to usurping his power. Indeed, he would have been delighted in seeing me employ his ways and play out life's roles in his well-calculated fashion, and in accordance with his directions, which unbeknownst to me were already perfectly etched in my unconscious. But since I was convinced I knew all about life's screenplay, I felt no compunction about refusing his influence. I was also bound by emotional conflict, and I distorted the perspective sufficiently away from the limits of proper to further confuse myself. Had I been more in touch with my feelings, I might have seen the meaning of the old saw, "Imitation is the sincerest form of flattery." Instead, I chose to believe that copying someone's style thwarted one's individuality, too blinded by the passions of youth to have seen beyond those infantile interpretations. Only time would remedy my misconceptions.

We placed the splintery chocks under the wheels of the airplane that day and went into the office to fill out the landing forms. We left

Bader Field Atlantic City Airport and went to the appointment at the home of a private client who had some fantastic paintings to sell. Instead of being fantastic, they were dreadful, so we stayed the polite amount of time and left at the first appropriate moment. We grabbed a leisurely lunch, which included the mandatory buckets of steamers followed by lobsters which had been steamed in seaweed.

"Hey Tad." I hated when he called me that. I looked up from the menu to his impish smirk.

"Yeah, Pop. What?"

"Aren't these steamers the best?"

"Yep, they're good all right."

"Don't forget the broth. It's the best part."

"I know, I know. Don't worry; I'll get to it."

Tad was such a diminutive word, I couldn't even look at Arlyn. But I got over it as I slurped the butter-laden clam broth and nodded in agreement. He was so right. This was a real taste treat; a feast for the senses, too short, but very sweet. It was time to head back to the airport; something I didn't want to do in the worst way. The conversation turned to business and how the upcoming year would be a challenge, but would stand us well in the long run. Even though the art markets looked deceptively optimistic, Pop warned of impending reversal.

"We need to be ready for the changing economic tide. We're at the end of an up cycle and 1974 is gonna crash." No one else shared his thinking, but I knew better than to challenge him. He'd been right too many times and I knew he'd be right this time too.

"Okay Pop, not to worry, we'll brace for the worst and get in position to quickly pick up the pieces of the others as they fall around us. We'll secure our cash position and sell off the lower end stuff fast and hold pat on the other." They would be surprised, we would be prepared.

It was growing a trifle sultry as the strong afternoon sun dissipated the remaining shade. Pop and I walked to the plane as Mom and Arlyn trailed behind. He put his arm around me as we walked.

"I'll be leaving for London in the morning."

"What?" I was taken aback. I would have known this days before. "When did this happen?"

"The deal just came across yesterday. No time to elaborate; I wanted to tell you in person. I'll be staying with Julius in London for a couple of days and then we're off to Switzerland to look at a jewel of a Renoir, a first rate Pissarro, and a couple of textbook Monets. It's all in a very private collection which is being sold quickly and with the utmost of discretion. If we get there by Tuesday, we can walk away with the whole deal!"

"Oh, okay, I get it." I understood his excitement as he divulged more of the details.

"Call the bank in the morning and make certain they arrange the necessary funding. There can be no delays or screw-ups, so stay on them and move fast."

"I'll call first thing tomorrow morning and get it done; no worries, Pop." I knew the limits of our credit and I also knew which way to go if we needed to reach beyond them, but it wouldn't be necessary for this deal.

We walked around the plane and did the standard checks before startup. We looked for prop nicks, dents or breaks along wing and aileron surfaces, both forward and aft, oil leaks, tire tread wear, and any other abnormal things we could find. Pop had filed a 3:50 flight plan so there was precious little time to waste. We hugged and kissed as they got on board.

"See you in the city, Mom," I said in a rather somber tone as I kissed her goodbye. Arlyn watched with pride as Pop and I hugged tightly and kissed one another goodbye.

"Thanks for lunch, Pop; the clams were incredible. Glad you came down. We had a great time. Be safe getting home and I'll see you when you get back from London. I love you!"

Time was short as they disappeared behind the tinted windshield. With the glaring sun, all that was visible was the eerie silhouette of Pop's face which was highlighted by the dark glasses and aura-like band of light around his head. I thought I saw him mouth the words, "I love you, too" just as the left engine began to crank.

A delicate puff of smoke and she kicked over, revving smoothly and waiting impatiently for number two to follow suit. A few twists, the belch of another white wisp and both engines were humming the tune of synchronization. The visual testing protocol would follow and the Aztec would be on her way to distant skies. A quick but affectionate wave of the hand, a thrown kiss, and they taxied toward the runway. I watched as the wings nodded left and right on their stroll down the concrete taxiway. They held briefly at the end, just short of the runway, to run up the engines. After all signs indicated the go ahead, they lined up on the asphalt path and the twin Lycomings roared at full throttle pulling them quickly to the point where they gracefully lifted off the ground, retracted the gear and climbed steeply into the brilliant but hazy blue sky.

I was overcome by an uneasy feeling that instantly enveloped me. I felt a terrible sadness, a total loneliness. Suddenly, I was filled with a queasy sense of being really alone for the first time in my life. It was more than uncomfortable—I couldn't shake it. I knew that the beads of sweat on my skin and the slight light-headedness I was experiencing were not at all attributable to the oppressive heat, but to a much more powerful force. I was intuitive enough to know that something was terribly wrong, but I couldn't have predicted what the next few days would bring. I only felt a dreaded vacancy that hadn't been there before today. I never expected to realize my worst fear; that I had seen my father for the very last time.

Chapter Four

The Funeral

It was August 5, 1973, the day we had to bury Pop. The funeral was scheduled for 10 a.m. at Levine's on Broad Street. My stomach was a mess and I'd been floating in and out of reality.

"Carl, please take one of these," Mom begged. "It's just a very mild tranquilizer; it'll calm you down." I wasn't big on drugs of any kind—perhaps an occasional aspirin or antibiotic when all else failed—but this time I felt it would get me through the events of this dreaded day.

"Okay, I'll take one." I suppose it helped, but I didn't notice the effect of this miraculous substance designed to dull or numb emotions.

The black stretch limousine was waiting downstairs in front of Mom's apartment. Arm in arm, we escorted her off the elevator and through the manned front door into the signature transport. In an all too brief twenty minutes we arrived at the funeral parlor. Mom,

Alan, Arlyn, and I had the option of seeing Pop one last time in a private viewing room before his casket was closed for good. Alan and Mom chose to view his body; I declined. To look at his lifeless shell was too painful. I needed to remember him in life as I'd known him; the vital force of energetic spirit who had become my hero through my years. I knew that if I'd taken that final look, that's what I would see every time I thought about him. Life was for living and I would go on with the strength of the memories that we'd built together.

There were hordes of people coming in to pay their respects. The crowds swelled into the street as the doors bulged with his honor. Friends, family, business acquaintances, and even nearby strangers were drawn by the hundreds to partake in this farewell to a dignitary, a head of state; even if the political system hadn't recognized him. Everyone who had come in contact with him either directly or indirectly would reverberate with the tremendously hollow vacuum in their lives as the soul known as Sam David left for higher grounds. My only regret was that his stay here was too brief. The onslaught of respect payers was so persistent, the eulogy was piped through the hallways and lobby so that those who couldn't squeeze through were able to partake in Pop's memorial.

Rabbi Martin Zion, who was Pop's best friend, performed the eulogy which was stunningly beautiful. I don't know how he made it through without breaking down. The flow of tears never ceased in the chapel that morning. After the service, endless lines of people expressed their condolences to us. It was very rewarding to see the immeasurable reach of his omniscient love.

There was a fellow waiting for the next funeral to start who heard Rabbi Martin's remarkable dedication. Arlyn was standing near him. "Who was this man?" he asked to no one in particular. "I wish I'd known him. What a special person he must have been."

Arlyn nodded, "He was very special, unique...one of a kind."

As we rode in the limousine to the cemetery, we began to recount the wonderful and silly experiences we'd shared with Pop as a family. They were too numerous to gather but many stood out in our minds and gave us great comfort. Too many families would never have the reward of such unconditional love, friendship, and warmth that we were fortunate enough to have enjoyed. We would continue to live life as soon as we felt ready. That is what he would have wanted for us; to take every day to the fullest with no regrets in the end. I took great solace in knowing that even though he wasn't in the physical, he was within reach in the spirit world.

It took an uneasy thirty minutes to get to the burial grounds where so many empty shells lay silently at rest. The labyrinth of concrete and limestone monuments was confusing. After a bit, they all looked the same, only the names changed. Amidst a row of ordinary headstones and grave markers a miniature skyscraper built in special recognition of some lost soul would occasionally protrude skyward. Seemed like a perfect waste of time and money, but I would never presume to impose my beliefs onto anyone else.

Tires crunched on the narrow gravel pathways as they twisted and turned. Soon, we arrived at the final destination where my father's vacated body would be interred.

Opening the doors, Alan said, "Here we go."

"Are you okay, Mom?"

"I'm all right," she whispered softly as she steadied herself, holding onto Alan on one side and me on the other. We walked to the dark green tent covering the newly dug grave. The casket was placed on leveraged straps that would lower it into the concrete housing below after we left.

There was a brief service with Rabbi Zion at the helm administering the traditional prayers and a brief but lovely final farewell to a great man. The sun was pitching its warmth upon us and all was silent. Then, we heard the wonderfully familiar sound of a twin- engine airplane circling directly overhead. It was a harmonious sound that only Aztecs made; there was no mistaking it. Looking upward into the most blue of late summer skies, was a red and white Aztec. Mom, Arlyn, and I instinctively looked at one another, nodded with acknowledgment and smiled with tears in our eyes. It was Pop and we knew it with more confidence than we'd ever known anything in our lives. He wouldn't have missed his own funeral. He was obviously a master of projecting his consciousness. As quickly as the Aztec above had appeared, it vanished. Then, a few moments later, it reappeared. My family acknowledged it as an ever-consoling presence of my father.

In the limo on the way back to Mom's apartment, I blurted, "It was Pop, you know—in the Aztec."

"I know," she agreed. "I saw it. He was there. I could feel him."

"Yep, it was Pop all right. Can you believe it, an Aztec overhead at the cemetery? How incredible is that? If that isn't a message, I don't know what is!" That is one presentation that I will never forget; it was stunningly real!

In those days, I had no notion of "living dreams" as they are called, but I was well aware of what they meant. Pop was telling us not to feel bad. He was free and still flying, but he'd be on his own as he made his way to a better place. The crushing pain of his major coronary was merely a release from the binding grasp of the physical which imposed its limits according to the laws of this worldly dimension. We would meet again in a much freer environment. There is no such thing as death; only a change in form as we leave one world and enter another. The only remnants are the fleshly bodies that identified the soul which resided within. The body is a vehicle for movement, for gathering of earthly experiences, for a full range of emotions, for a total collection of situations, obstacles, and solutions as they are overcome. It is the building which houses our black box; a permanent record of events and lessons that will be taken to the next worlds as we are ready to enter them for the continuation of our education. The curriculum never ends; it just changes format with each accumulation of knowledge from the preceding realm.

Chapter Five

Picking Up the Pieces

I had two very critical situations to face without the slightest notion of how to handle either of them. The first one dealt with Mom who had just taken a knockout punch so deeply that none of us were sure she would survive it. Mom had undergone the crippling loss of a son (my older brother, Bruce), and now the devastating loss of her husband. How much could this remarkable woman endure?

Bruce was at the age of twenty-three—a marvelous mixture of rugged adventure and deep sensitivity. He was the sweet essence of everything a parent could wish for in a child. Loved by everyone for his golden warmth, revered by many for his looming six-foot stature, his presence illuminated the paths of those who were fortunate enough to cross it. His charisma was magnetic. Not as New England as the Kennedy variety, but just as compelling with its refreshing innocence. He was a typical sixties teenager with the fast hot rod, dashing blue eyes, and rippling muscular build. His movie idol appearance was complete with the proverbial flip top box of Marlboro's tucked under his neatly pressed short-sleeved, whiter-than-white cotton vee-neck tee shirt. His hair—neither wavy nor straight, but a bit crimped in its light to medium brownish flavor—adorned his slightly angular face. Scarcely an ounce of fat to be found anywhere, but a wealth of power surrounding those magnificent generous bones. The girls all but beat down the doors to get to him. The phone rang with no end. Every girl said, "Hi Bruce. What are you doing? Wanna come over and keep me company? I'm sooo lonely." The females connived for his company or at least for the comfort of his soothing voice. They swooned around him like a teen idol and hated to be cast away in rejection because they had gotten there too late. They accepted their fate with dignity knowing that another day would come and—like the lottery—they might win their chance with him. It wasn't just his magnificent all-American boy look that drove them wild with passion; it was his general makeup as a human being. His warmth and compassion embraced like the lick of a puppy dog. He was affectionate and loving, and though sometimes a tease, he was genuine. He was sympathetic and caring in both a childlike and grown-up fashion, never seeming to have a care in the world.

From my younger vantage point, life in his world was scattered with fun and excitement. He had little to worry about except curfews and allowances. I perceived his most difficult task was deciding which girl to take out first, and how to tell the rest of his swooning adorers with a sense of diplomacy that he wasn't available. I was merely a teenager myself and wore the standard frustrations that went along with the virgin territory. I didn't realize there were real problems in the world which had to be confronted and that life was really more than girls and cars and school. As any teenager, he was immersed in the hedonistic pleasures of the all-consuming present. We worried about how many gallons of gas we could get for a dollar, and which local hang out to cruise. There were two Hot Shoppes, one which we frequented and another in a remote neighborhood which harbored a very tough crowd. Everyone would congregate on weekend evenings to show off their "souped up" cars and hopefully pick up blonde girls wearing tight jeans. Would we wind up cruising all night going home empty, or luckily find love after thoroughly searching for that tightly sweater-wrapped female with cascading, finely combed hair that held the essence of her perfume and submissive eyes whose gaze locked into ours at first sight and drew us together in that instant? The dream of making out with a nubile female whose soft pouting lips opened with invitation in the back seat of that summertime Detroit iron was usually just that, a dream. But on occasion, our flesh would glisten with goose bumps and a cool breeze as we'd find ourselves in that idyllic situation and savor the reward that would turn into an enriching memory to be recalled at will.

Bruce

Issues of concern were whose car was faster and which one made the most threatening noise? Dual exhausts, lake pipes, if you were among the chosen scarce few to have a Vette. Holley carburetors were

BADER FIELD

the rage, especially when they were coupled with the GTO or 442 packages. There were the deep rumblings of the '57 Chevys and of course the '57 T-Birds. Once in a harvest moon you would even get to glimpse a Sunbeam Tiger which looked and sounded as if it could fly. "Wow, he must be really rich." Echoed the drooling oohs and aahs. It hid an enormous Ford power block in the swollen belly of its tiny body, which was practically weightless when measured against everything else lumbering along the streets of summer. We were in the midst of a generation of screeching tires, rumbling exhausts, Mag wheels, and convertibles. It seemed like the guys with the slickest machines had the best looking girls beside them. If you had the first, the second was almost a given. There were even designated places for street racing, like Delaware Avenue at midnight, the Boulevard, if you were there and were challenged, or maybe a vacant avenue was a perfect staging area for that particular evening. The police were wise to most of this nonsense, but if we were careful, brief in our flagrance, and a bit lucky, we might avoid their peering eyes altogether.

The bowling alley was another favorite hangout for the "cool" set, and there were bonus points if you could bowl well. Bruce had natural athletic ability and turned in scores in the middle 200's more often than not. He was immeasurably successful at the fun things in life, and wasn't particularly fascinated by the family art business. He preferred to go with the creative flow of his own artistic sense. He possessed a divine mechanical aptitude which would've brought him enormous success if it had been given proper channeling. Many times I had watched in awe as he dismantled what appeared to be the most complex mechanisms of the automobile engine, make corrections for improved performance, and then re-assemble it in its entirety without so much as a manual. I was astonished that he knew exactly when and where everything was to be placed, and with surgical precision. It was impressive to observe such an operation; so much so that I learned nearly everything I know today from those casual observations. He could make the roughest running engine simmer down to a silent and rhythmic calm at the mere adjustment of a mixture valve or idle screw. It wasn't just that he knew the technical aspects so well, it was that he could feel in his soul what needed to be done. It was instinctive, not tedious, or labored.

The dark green '54 Mercury was a story in itself. Bruce picked it up for a song because it needed some work and the owner didn't have the time or the patience to make it run the way the factory had right out of the box. Out would come a staggering array of tools and the powder blue chamois cloth on which he arranged them like pieces in a symphony. Each would have their designated role and would be on call until the process was finished. Up went the hood and the work began swiftly and methodically with no talk other than the gentle bell and twang sounds of metal against metal. After about a day and a half of replacement and alteration of worn out parts, Bruce was ready for all challengers. From outward appearances the car looked precisely the same until the engine was cranked up. It rumbled with a dare me vibration that told of the racing cam which lurked beneath that unassuming dark green exterior. It wasn't just noise, it was a tuned thunder, even at idle, which had been accomplished by opening up the exhaust system and eliminating the resonators after installing state-of-the-art glass-packed mufflers. The sound was awesome and can only be understood by experiencing the excitement of a cigarette type powerboat boasting twin 454 Magnums and a flow through exhaust system. If you haven't heard one of them close up, or have no feel what I am trying to describe, take a trip to the nearest marina and hang around until you hear one of those boisterous bastions of speed start up and lurch to the sea.

The '54 Mercury was relatively tame unless excessive acceleration was applied. Not only did the car take off as if it wore wings, it sounded the part as well. The most outlandish ear punishment occurred upon back down, and that was the time when none of us who were inside the car could hold back the laughter. Even from inside it sounded as if there had just been a barrage of machine gun fire released from all directions. Bruce would wait patiently for crowds of people to stand on the street corners. He would drive by peacefully and then suddenly burst full speed ahead with increasing velocity. Then, he would ease off the gas pedal altogether. We derived a perverse sense of pleasure in seeing everyone jump as if there were an unexpected explosion under their feet. They looked around in awe, dumbstruck by what had just flown by; some even ducked and hit the ground fearing their next moments. I suppose you had to be there to appreciate it, but it gave us countless hours of good times and memories. It also landed Bruce quite a few tickets for noise abatement violations, but it was worth it.

A short time afterward, I guess the thrill had worn off, or maybe it got to be too costly, but Bruce sold the car. He had the insight to know that real serious work was just around the next corner if he kept it, so he gave it to the gas station to sell for him. Their parking lot was perfectly situated across from the Hot Shoppe and within a few days, it was sold for a profit. As soon as the new owner took possession and drove off the parking lot, the drive shaft fell out.

The next set of wheels was a bright yellow checker cab which cost Bruce the extraordinary sum of fifty dollars. The cab company was getting rid of the old fleet in favor of some newer vehicles with more modernized equipment, so we rushed down to one of the worst neighborhoods in North Philadelphia, "The Badlands" as we knew it, to retrieve the newest addition to the David family. There were only about a dozen of them left; I guess the rest had been sold, stolen, or scavenged for parts. We got into the cab, grateful that the door locks still worked. It was almost dark and it was time to get the hell out of there. We prayed it would start. It did, and we made a quick and inconspicuous exit.

We got flagged down about six times on the way home. When Mom saw this taximobile as we pulled up to the front of the house, she politely pointed. We knew her gesture meant that we would not dare park such an embarrassing vehicle of in the front of the house. What would the neighbors think? It looked like a banana with wheels, and besides you would never know when someone would be brazen enough to knock on your door and ask for a ride. Sure enough, old ladies would flag Bruce down and then curse him out after he'd pass them by empty. Mom and Pop couldn't stand it anymore, and they gave him a real automobile.

Bruce was a free spirit by nature. But, his very nature must also have caused him untold internal strife. It just wasn't in keeping with the family tradition to drift effortlessly with no particular direction. Organization of one's life was perpetually stressed on the home front. Definitive action and success were necessary partners in a symbiotic marriage. Idle time was acceptable in its proper perspective, but as a general practice, it was viewed as being detrimental to one's advancement in life. To say the least, Bruce was uncertain as to what to do with the rest of his life. Moreover, the Army had been breathing down his back with repeated rumors of an impending voyage to Vietnam. The newspapers were filled with reports of casualties and disaster, so the promise of visiting the war-ravaged land of Southeast Asia posed a frightening nightmare to Bruce. He enlisted in the Army reserves for the six-month program which offered a weekend per month stay at a nearby base after boot camp. The overall hitch was something like six years, after which the obligation was over whether or not you had been called for active duty. It was kind of a lottery situation which more often than not went no further than the weekend warrior bit, but the news was growing worse by the day and tensions were rising as fears mounted. Units were still being sent over with frightening regularity to certain disaster with less than pessimistic odds of returning with all of their components intact.

The picture was clouded with gloom and the media was producing a constant barrage of pictures of bloodied villages with countless casualties on both sides. The chances of Bruce's unit being overlooked were really slim, and there could be no guarantees as to what the future held. His unit was on alert and was on standby for mobilization. He was paralyzed by a vice-like grip of fear as the media continued to deliver its payload of armaments to the tax-paying public in the guise of sensationalism.

Concurrently, college, which might have given Bruce the option of a deferment from the military, had been a bone of contention. It just couldn't provide him with the necessary emotional stimulation that his parched artistic spirit required. And yet, to discard the academic path to suit his needs for gratification would surely have been perceived as a self-damning experience. It was not as though he didn't try; he went to Temple University for a while, and then to its night school, but apparently he suffered from the same learning difference that I apparently inherited. He was trapped; locked into a corner which seemed to have no exit. In his mind, one direction would lead him to failure while the other would deem him a failure. The battle within him was raging like a forest fire that spread uncontrolled.

I awoke to get ready for school one crisp morning in mid-October. There was a very strong feeling of malaise in the house that day. None of us had slept for some reason.

"Where's Bruce?" I asked at breakfast.

"Bruce didn't come home last night." Mom and Pop's nervous refrain echoed. It was not like him to simply disappear and not inform anyone of his whereabouts.

"Maybe he stayed with Helen."

"We called her; he wasn't there. She hasn't heard a word from him and she is very uneasy."

The level of anxiety in the house was increasing, but I had to go to school. I hadn't a clue as to where Bruce had been the night before. What if something had happened to him? What if he was hurt and there was no one there to help him? What if.......

I arrived at school about fifteen minutes later, parked out front on Ogontz Avenue and climbed up the south lawn where everybody congregated at lunchtime to smoke and catch the midday sunshine. I walked through the front doors to the auditorium for morning assembly. Although my head wasn't entirely there, I fell into the morning clatter with my friends. I had barely been seated when the vice-principal called, "Carl David, come to the stage."

A gray chill shattered my sixteen-year-old body. My mouth dried to the point where it was useless and nearly impossible to swallow. My vision dimmed as my eyes were squeezed tightly into the back of my head. The pounding in my chest was deafening. Once I reached the stage, I froze with anticipation of what I would hear.

Mr. Carlisle leaned down to me. "You are to go directly home; there has been an emergency." I heard his words but they weren't sinking in to my mind. My legs jellied and I felt like I was going to black out. This couldn't really be happening; it was a bad dream. I ran to the car scrambling for my keys which were in my back pocket. I yanked them out with a pile of tissues that flew into the street. Rushing frantically, I shook as I inserted the key into the door lock. I jerked the door open, jumped in the driver's seat, and started the engine in one motion. With dreaded anticipation, I started the eternally long ten-minute trip home. I was intuitive enough to know that something awful had happened. My mind whirled. Was Bruce in a car accident? Had he had been in a fight? Did he get shot? The school had withheld information to which I felt entitled, but I was grateful that they had the decency not to tell me. Perhaps that action was the order of Mom and Pop or maybe it was standard practice under emergency situations, but in any case, I dreaded facing the news that awaited me at our house. I slammed the car into park, ripped the keys out of the ignition, tore up three front steps, burst through the door, and ran inside.

Alan was waiting for me by the stairs. "Bruce is dead. He hanged himself in the gallery last night."

I would never be able to erase his pronouncement. The words reverberated in my head as they bounced off of every wall of our home. I deafened at the repugnant message. My eyes filled with pain and disbelief. I leaped up the steps to get to Mom. She was in her bedroom with Aunt Ethel by her side. I ran to her and held her but I was unable to speak. She looked at me pathetically and mortally wounded, "Why? Why? Why?"

We shared tears of pain and anguish the likes of which I didn't know existed. A knife had slashed our picture-perfect canvas of life to shreds. Blinded by the mortality of our loved one, we were lowered to the bottom of the depths of sadness where no light could enter or escape. I was in a state of shock as I walked to my room down the hall and shut the door. I wanted to be alone, maybe forever. I had never imagined even the possibility of such harsh blackness. It was too ripping to have been real, and yet it was just that—a reality with which we would have to come to grips. I don't know how Alan could even have told me. It must have been a horror for him to have to break that news to me. It was painful enough just to endure hearing it let alone to have to share it with another loved one.

Pop had walked into the gallery that morning with a good deal of fear in his heart, only to find his son suspended from the rafters.

The image of his lifeless body hunched over and limp as the hand-fashioned braided rope noose snuffed out his last breath. It was a godforsaken nightmare that etched a permanent scar in his mind as it did in mine, and I didn't even see it. Hearing about it was torturous enough.

When he had discovered the stiffened lifeless body of his child in the "shop" as it was referred to in those days, Pop first called Mom's sister, Annabelle. Sobbing to her on the telephone, he didn't know how to tell Mom, and didn't want her to be alone when she found out what had happened. The police were summoned, as well as some very close friends of the family, and it finally all exploded into the open. A shockwave was issued and felt everywhere within and without the community. People were wonderful to us. Their sympathy and comfort was overwhelmingly outpoured, and was received with great appreciation.

My father was desolate. When he returned to the house that morning, we were all together except for Bruce. He came into my room and we held each other for support. We spoke no words for there were none that could mean anything. Anything said would have trivialized the horrible loss we both embraced in each other. Unspoken words were far more expressive; we lived the agony and the defeat. We would talk later. Bruce's battle was over, but ours had just begun. Pop suffered a loss so great that he carried it to his grave with him. Bruce and I were as close as two humans could ever be. The memory of his anguish will remain a pathetic and permanent relic of my teenage years. The unparalleled image of my brother had been shattered. Somehow I was convinced that the whole thing was a horrible mistake. It couldn't be real. For years afterward, I even fantasized that Bruce had become involved in some governmental espionage plot, and that he was alive and well in some foreign country with a new identity. I tried in vain to avoid the harsh pain of reality. It forced itself upon me as I realized there would be no more trips together to the Willow Grove Air Force Base to watch the jets scream to altitude and do their maneuvers while we were fasting on the highest of Jewish holidays. Washing the cars together in the summertime sun was now a thing of the past. No more wrestling and fighting and teasing; all that would be put away for good. No more fishing trips to the shore where we used to venture on Saturday morning. We would rent a garvy, take it out in the bay, and haul in endless dozens of freshly-caught blowfish that Bruce would later convert into a fish salad. The games of stickball at the schoolyard would have to be retired or painfully shared with other partners. Life would never be the same. Bruce had taken with him more lives than his own.

Alan had his own special attachment to Bruce for they were only three years apart. His suffering was great, but he kept it to himself through many darkened years. Alan's sense of loss for Bruce was much deeper than his façade reflected. I cannot forget my tear-streaked words to him at the time when the funeral was over and all of the company had gone home to their own families. We were in our room, in our beds, with the lights turned off, with a giant gulf in our hearts. I turned to him and made a profoundly difficult statement which I barely choked out of my throat. "It's just you and me now, Alan." We cried together in our new found unity. We were each immersed in our own swirling pools of agony, unable to shed the horror. It was like a recurring nightmare from which we were unable to escape, because when awakened, the reality was the same as the dream.

Through the darkness, Pop was the pillar of strength for all of us. Mom had just come out of the hospital and was recovering from major surgery when Bruce died, so Pop had to shove his own grief aside to lend her the will to live. He was a very brave man—a fighter with the exceptional ability to withstand defeat, and continue down life's so very unpredictable path. Somehow he gave the outward impression of a superhuman being unscathed on the front lines of the world's toughest battlefield. But, at night the truth came out. I could hear the faint sounds of weeping coming from my parent's bedroom. I couldn't even imagine the pain they shared. To lose a brother is horrific, but to lose a child is far worse. There is no worse horror for a parent than losing a child—the ultimate gift of God which they loved from the instant of its creation as it was formed from a mixture of passion and deep love—the very essence of one's own flesh and blood; nursed like a piece of your own soul.

The radiance was gone from Mom and Pop's faces. Their speech was vacant words without happiness, but life had to go on. Our family lived with the eternal and persistent question "why?" Perhaps we'd never know why he had perpetrated such a violent and final end to his seemingly happy life. As people continued to hear of the unspeakable event that shook our world, they offered consolations of great comfort. But like a double-edged sword, it re-energized the pain all over again. Our agony was but a memory away and the loneliness surfaced at the hint of anything related to Bruce. Every time someone who knew him crossed our path, the wound would fester and weep. Mid-October would forever be a time of remembrance. July 26 had been a day of celebration—Bruce's birthday—now the day only brings emptiness to our hearts.

Mom struggled with the eternal vacancy day by day, wondering if she would survive or if she even wanted to. The gravity of the blackness was beyond anything she'd ever experienced; it was unearthly, inhuman, of despicable evil. And yet, she knew that she had two other children and a husband who would need her now more than ever. The battle was fierce, but she found a previously unknown inner strength and mustered every bit of fight left in her to forge onward and overcome the depths of her pain to survive this mortal wound. She wrapped herself in the bandages of life, changing the dressings with every waking moment, determined not to surrender to the tempting pull of depression. She had to stay focused on moving forward, but it took everything she had to journey one day at a time. Her endless nights were flooded with nightmares. At each dawn, she waged the same daunting and unrelenting war hoping to achieve small victories. She had no battle plan or precedent upon which she could rely, no mapped out strategy for success, no telling of the outcome. Her close circle of family and friends strode alongside her gradual recovery as the pain ebbed and flowed with a tide-like rhythm. The cycles eventually widened, bringing more daylight than darkness as time slowly patched the wound.

Pop blamed himself for not having seen it coming. He knew that Bruce's forte was not academics and he supported him in every endeavor. Bruce was amazingly skilled with his hands; his mechanical ability was beyond superior. Pop was the one to find his middle son suspended from the rafters on the fourth floor of the gallery—the very place that Pop had planned to set up a frame shop so Bruce could design and fashion frames for the inventory. Pop was unable to return to the fourth floor of the gallery for years; the very thought sickened him. Pop would have done anything to make sure his son was happy. From all outward appearances, he was happy, carefree, easy going, and simply delightful. But underneath that smiling façade must have been smoldering an abnormal level of distress that went totally undetected. Like Pop, Bruce was quite adept at hiding whatever was wreaking havoc within his psyche. No one had a clue of his lack of an avenue to vent his frustration, but it must have been an intolerable mixture of life elements that exploded in one final destructive act.

Pop couldn't blame his son; that would be equal to treason and would jeopardize his unconditional love for Bruce, which was all that was left save for the memories. Instead, Pop covered his pain with a defensive shield of anger that served as an emotional wall as he forged ahead blindly into his work at the gallery. His dark glasses ineffectively attempted to hide his rage and distress buried just beneath the surface. In the weeks and months following Bruce's death, Pop would burst through the gallery door, slamming it behind him with enough contempt to shake the building, but not enough though to clear the history that had become a part of our shattered heritage. The entire tenor of the building had changed as it absorbed the horrific act of violence that fractured the once nearly idyllic David family.

Bruce's death traumatized me to such a degree that I didn't care about anything anymore. School had become an effort of monumental proportion. I had no clue what to do or where to go; I was a lost soul trying to wade through what once had been familiar corridors meandering toward the meaningless activities of each classroom. My heart carried a vile mixture of anger, disbelief, and embarrassment. I dreaded entering those hallowed halls every day. I was a spectacle. Surreptitious stares came from every direction.

"That's him, that's him—the one whose brother killed himself. Did you hear?" I heard their bellowing whispers. I felt like an outcast, no longer belonging in the mainstream. Some veered away as I approached, others managed an attempt at being polite, but no matter what, they all had the same thoughts on their minds. I was judged by their glares and their warped sense of guilt by association. I was sixteen and had just lost my closest friend. I was no longer the same person I was a couple of weeks before. I guess I even looked different. I definitely felt different. Some of my friends backed away from me as if I had contracted a disease, but fortunately most of the world was very understanding and compassionate.

When teachers asked for my work, I replied dimly, "I am not ready yet to do the homework." For a while, they accepted my resistance.

After a few weeks I regained a modicum of momentum with the support of some wonderful teachers like my French professor, Mr. Silberstein. I remember when he said, "Monsieur David, are you ready yet to get back into gear?" His words were kind and compassionate and his eyes filled with love as he awaited my answer. I welled up.

"Yes, I think I am. Thank you for your patience," my voice cracked as I tried to restrain the tears. I was willing to take his assignments. He was a kind man and a great teacher. I learned to speak fluent French in his class. I can still see his face and feel his gaze upon me as he would cast an invisible copious look my way to make sure I was okay.

I gently slid back into the cracks of society to the point that only I could see the scars which nothing would ever be able to remove. My close friends were still my friends, and gratefully didn't treat me any differently than before. They did have a deep understanding when I wasn't in a very festive mood, or if I chose not to tag along when I was feeling down. I still remember the guys and the girls who came to see me at the house when we were sitting shiva, "We are so sorry, is there anything we can do?" I couldn't contain the tears when they showed up on my behalf. There was an incredible bond of friendship between us which was only strengthened with the warmth in their being there. We cherished the notes of condolence from the kids at school and the teachers and administrative staff as well. It was an aspect of comfort which both pleased and saddened me, and one which I hadn't expected.

I went on fitfully to graduate high school and planned with a degree of resignation to attend Temple University. It was close to home and a large group of my friends were going there as well. I entered in 1966 and struggled my way through the huge factory of students who sat in clusters of 300 at the various seminars as the professors threw their banks of boring knowledge at us and expected memorization and regurgitation of the same verbiage months later during final exam period. It was a really disgraceful attempt at imparting information to us. I would have done better not attending and just reading the text books instead. I had a terrible time with the art history course which was vital if I were to enter the family business in the years ahead. French literature was impossible, and I was fluent in French. But in the long run it was Geology that brought me down. At the end of the year, after basically teaching myself the course because the teacher had no talent in getting the point across, I failed the final exam. The teacher would not cut me any slack. He wouldn't even consider my classroom participation, which was luminary, and though my average was hovering on the C/D line, he wouldn't give me the benefit of the doubt. He sadistically gave me a "D" for the year. At that point, I threw in the hat. I didn't need any more grief. I was ready to quit and just go to work. I didn't know what else to do.

I was in bed one Saturday morning just after the whole mess at school had transpired when the mail came and Mom brought a letter upstairs to me.

"It's from Temple University. These must be your grades honey," she smiled.

"Nope, it's my eviction notice. They have thrown me out for failing to maintain a minimum grade point average." I began to shake with worry as I wondered what my father would do. I had disappointed him and had absolutely no idea how angry he would be with my failure. When he got home from work that Saturday morning, he walked in to my room. He already knew—the look on his face was evidence of that—but it wasn't one of anger or disappointment.

"Hey," he pulled back the bedcover I was hiding under. "Don't fret, we're gonna get you reinstated first and then we'll get you out of there. This is the wrong school for you. It's too big. You need a place where you can learn, not a factory where you have to teach yourself."

I should not have been surprised at Pop's compassion throughout my college transition. He'd just lost one son and undoubtedly placed blame squarely on his shoulders. It didn't belong there, but what parent wouldn't feel responsible for his child's demise? I should have known he'd go to the ends of the universe for any one of us. And, although his smile was tarnished with a wound so deep it would never heal, the inner essence of his love would always shine through for us. I was in need and he was without question there for me. I never had to ask; it was always there and given before I even knew I needed it.

Carl and Pop College Days

Pop got me reinstated and my record sponged of disgrace. Then, he informed the university that I would not be returning in the fall. He scrambled, pulled strings, and used all his connections to get me into a host of schools around the country. Mom and Pop felt that I needed to get away from home to escape a difficult past and grow up, but I never wanted to leave home. My high school transcripts were forwarded to the American College Admissions Center—an organization which for a flat fee of $300 would only send them to colleges and universities where the odds of acceptance were excellent. I began receiving invitations and acceptances to many colleges, and wound up going to Oglethorpe College in Atlanta. It was my first time away from home, and I performed beautifully for two years by making Dean's list and Spanish Honor Society from the first semester to the end.

The day I left with Alan to drive my stuff down to school was a tear-filled one for me, but I couldn't let him see my pain. I feared ridicule, though it probably never would have manifested. My head was writhing with masses of irrational thoughts. I was headed for the unknown once again. This time the experience would not be wrought with pain and despair; it would be a clean slate upon which I hoped to regain my identity.

For the rest of his days, Pop bore the brunt of the responsibility. Consumed by his guilt, he was convinced that Bruce had aimed this final desperate act toward him. He couldn't comprehend the situation for its most unpleasant truth, which was simply Bruce's inability to cope with life. Instead, he chose to believe, as most parents would, that it was entirely his fault, and not related to the attendant fragility of his son's innermost psyche. That burden grew less dominant in the remaining years of Pop's life, but it never retired. It was transformed into a more amorphous beast which left a distinct mark on his personality. He became more and more engrossed in his work; six and seven days a week, and nights as well. It was as if he was going to find solace in working himself to exhaustion—perhaps to death.

Some fathers would probably have placed distance between themselves and their other children after such a horrid experience, perhaps thinking they were preventing a repeat occurrence, but Pop did precisely the opposite. He developed new bonds of closeness with us to fill the void created by Bruce's death. We all shared the same insecurities and welcomed that extra touch of concern. Pop became significantly more protective of us, but I think that it only increased our closeness and consideration for one another. It really wasn't inconvenient to call Mom and Pop if the hour was growing late and we weren't going to be home on time, or if there was a change of plans which would carry us to a different location than originally slated. In the beginning, there were no late nights away from home. The worry and tension in their faces and hearts was too much to bear. We needed to be there with them as much as they needed us there, and though Bruce would never be there with us again, he would always be there in spirit.

I had to survive for my own sake but even more so for Mom and Pop. As selfish as I wanted to be, I had to sacrifice my own despair to help them move forward. It took years before the laughter returned to my father's life. At first it was tinged with uncertainty and bridled with restraint, but after a while it seemed to echo its former carefree style. Pop aged quickly in a way that was not overtly recognizable except to those of us who really knew the man. The inner regions of his eyes disclosed the penetrating pain, and reflected his fear of the future, which until Bruce's demise, wouldn't have been given a second thought.

Chapter Six

Filling Pop's Shoes

Pop had been dead for a few months. The days were growing shorter and the hot weather had lost its punch. There were but a few periods when the daily temperature would break sixty degrees. I had gotten very busy in the gallery trying to survive while making a serious attempt at living again.

Mom came to gallery early one morning with a package under her left arm and her pocketbook beneath her right arm. She extended her arm to hand me the package which was shrouded in tissue paper and then neatly arranged in a nondescript plastic bag.

She looked at me with as much directness as she could muster and quietly uttered, "This is for you—I know you will appreciate them, and that they'll fit. I know how much sentiment they hold."

I hadn't the vaguest idea what was beyond the outer layers of this mysterious presentation. I reluctantly reached for it and said thank you out of habit. I peeled back the crinkled edges of the plastic and stuck my hand in to feel the contents. I grabbed something solid under the tissue paper and pulled it out.

"Oh my God," I murmured to myself, quietly. *These are the shoes Pop bought just before he died. He never even had the chance to wear them. They were his favorites.*

I filled up with tears, but tried to hide them from Mom. I didn't want to upset her any more than she already was. I knew that seeing these shoes, let alone, giving them to me, was very painful for her. I also knew that there would be a sense of relief for her in getting them out of her apartment, which in turn made me wonder how difficult it would be for her when she recognized them on my feet instead of Pop's.

This was a very strange and delicate experience for me. Every adage of "filling the shoes" and "following in the footsteps" surfaced and struck me squarely in the face. The next challenge was Cinderella-like; I had to see if they fit. They were my size, and I admired the sleek dark cordovan Italian leather. I tried the left one on first. It fit like a glove. I put the right one on next. It too fit like a glove. They weren't exactly comfortable, but they were Pop's, and though they could never really be mine, walking in them gave me a sense of connection to him. They were an heirloom in a funny sort of way. I felt that donning his shoes would afford me the power, respect, and recognition, which he had earned, and in a deeper sense, keep him alive until they wore out. I wondered whether or not I would go so far as to resole them or even replace the heels when the originals gave out. At first blush, I thought unquestionably that I would, even if it meant the ruination of my feet. I imagined myself sleeping in them and hoping they would sustain the daily saturation of my morning shower.

Chapter Seven

Flying

Not too long after Pop's death, I was in the gallery one afternoon. It had been quiet that day and I wasn't really in the mood to do much, and I couldn't get airplanes off my mind. No matter what I did to change the subject in my head, the images returned with greater persistence. I could hear them taking off with their engines pulsing at full tilt as they zoomed overhead. Whether real or imagined, I could even smell kerosene as the vapors of the distantly departed jets drifted lazily in our direction. All this prompted me to make the telephone call to Atlantic Aviation. I would have to pay a visit to Bader Field. Bader Field is in Atlantic City and was used as the primary vehicle (other than by automobiles and trains) for bringing people into the area. It was, I believe, the oldest airfield in America and was named after the Mayor of Atlantic City. We kept the Aztec 6897 Yankee at Philadelphia International Airport in their general aviation facility, (Atlantic Aviation) adjacent to the main terminals.

As I was driving to the hangar that afternoon, I began to recall all the times I had been there in the past. It had been my way of life for so many years. The action had always been nonstop even into the wee hours of the evening with people on their way to somewhere, or on their return from another place. From the air, the lights glittered below as the planes made their approach to Philadelphia International Airport. The surrounding oil tanks winked harmoniously a thousand fold each second. There must have been a hundred thousand incandescent watts burning brightly and lighting the ground as though it were daylight. The headlights of the passing automobiles targeted the roads ahead of them and gave the appearance of dual flashlights moving evasively in random direction. When they streamed together it was like looking at a mammoth ray of light that was seemingly unbreakable, until a few dissidents turned off onto another roadway to form their own beam of guidance. The refineries worked around the clock so there was always a sense of life and action. The blow-off from the gas processors fountained into the sky with brilliant orange illumination as the flames leapt upward, sometimes as much as twenty and thirty feet. They would perform gloriously for a second or two, then retreat, and then repeat the act with continuous enthusiasm, lighting the surrounding skies, then darkening them with their absence, then lighting them again, and again, and again.

From the ground, looking up one could spot the airplanes coming in for a landing as they were on final approach. Their landing lights could illuminate a football field to near reading level. They were blinding, but exciting to look upon as they approached, from a distant twinkle as they first identified themselves for descent, to the penetrating extraterrestrial rays they forwarded when nearing the runway. We used to try and guess what kind of aircraft would be next, as it was far afield on final. The more strobe lights and white lights, the more complicated the task. Their objective was to be seen clearly, and often the light they emitted was so dazzling that it was easier to identify them by the sounds they made rather than by their appearance. The drone of the thrust reversers was ear splitting as the thunderous wake of the Rolls Royce or Pratt and Whitney jet engines was redirected forward to resist the aircraft to a halt. They came in pretty hot and needed all the assistance available to stop eating up the runway. At the peak of the reversing emphasis you could hear the crackle in the air as if electricity were being shot through the sky. It was thrilling and frighteningly awesome.

Today would be my first solo endeavor into what had always been a partnership effort. It was totally my responsibility now and I wasn't at all thrilled with the prospect of going it alone. Pop was irretrievably gone and airplane upkeep was not of special interest to Alan. I had done my share of flying, having had a tenuous start when I was a shy six years of age, so I had a curious fondness for the metal birds.

The memories were wonderful. I remember when I worked up the nerve to let my father take me up and around the first time. It was at Morrisville Airport in Morrisville, Pennsylvania just north of Trevose. Those were the days when Pop would rent an airplane—well before owning one. The airport had a grass landing strip, no concrete runway, and no lights. It took hours and hours of zooming down the grass runway, lifting off about ten feet and coasting down again before I'd let him take off and do the complete pattern at six-hundred to eight-hundred feet. I was thoroughly terrified and am certain to this day that my fingernails left their imprint in the metal undercarriage of the seat of the old Tri-Pacer which Pop rented faithfully every Saturday and Sunday for years.

Unicom at Bader Field

He surely must have taken a generous amount of chiding and ridicule from the guys in the tower, such as it was; it was more like a small room with a Unicom (a two-way radio utilized by small airports that did not have a tower. Pilots could inquire of the active runway and winds, but traffic was done by visual means.) Usually there was one guy manning the unicom (radio) in a small smoke-filled room and guys knew all the pilots by first name. They couldn't possibly have imagined what the hell he was doing with all of those aborted takeoffs and landings. Pop would smile with assurance.

"That wasn't so bad was it?" he would question upon landing.

"No—not so bad," I choked out as I gasped a sigh of relief to be back on the ground. I trembled at his next inquiry to try it again, but I guess my feeling foolish was heavier than my fear of flying, so we did it again, and again, and again. That was the very shaky beginning of the years of veteran sky time with Pop.

For some reason, there are two specific flights which I remember indelibly. The first one, which effects a feeling of peacefulness, was the return trip in the Tri-Pacer, "44 Papa" from Trenton to Morrisville. We were cruising at about 4,500 feet, 140 knots, and it was about six o'clock on a rather summery day. There were no winds, and the sun was setting in the distance in front of us. We were near the airport, but the atmosphere was such that it felt as though the entire world had been put on hold. It stressed the absence of anything but tranquility, and it lasted forever, or at least for the forty-five minutes that followed. Rarely had I enjoyed such a calm anywhere else on or above the earth. Time was asleep, and I was privileged to have captured a segment of it from another perspective. The sun transformed itself from a glowing orange to a mature reddish amber as it slowly relaxed into the horizon. The rays above it, which criss-crossed throughout the once blue sky, were streaks of deep yellow, orange, and magenta; a wavelength of spectrum. The atmosphere was alive and rainbow-swept from one end to the other as far as the eye could see. As we peered eastward, we could see the edge of darkness creeping rapidly upon our path. The sinking globe of retired fire was nearly vanished into the earth, save for the rich pink tinged purple corona which was the last to yield to the next hemisphere. Suddenly darkness was minutes away and there was the runway in front of us. I was sad to have to let go of the experience, but it was one I would never forget.

The other flight, which wasn't nearly as fond a remembrance, took place on a Sunday afternoon when Pop was "going under the hood" for some training. That simply meant that he would be wearing a visor which would blind him to all but the instrument panel. He would have no visibility out of any window, thereby forcing him to live by the instruments. In reality, it was a simulation of zero visibility conditions outside, such as locked in fog or complete cloud cover. Pop was studying for his instrument rating, which was one of the most strenuous regimes in flight management that was ever invented. It meant countless hours of being under the hood, untold months of regulations and chart plotting, and basic training for flying in the blind. Norm Hortmann, his friend and instructor, was training him, and after a couple of hours in the back seat with Norm's unfiltered cigarette smoke drifting in my direction, I thought I was going to be sick. Pop couldn't see where he was going, and that petrified me, the smoke was vile, and the steep turn and bank procedures could wreak havoc with anyone's equilibrium. That wasn't beyond survival, but when we did touch and go practice and Norm killed one engine in the Apache just as we were pulling off the ground, I thought it was over for all of us. I thought he was being a wise guy, or worse yet, a complete idiot with a very weird sense of humor. As it turns out, that technique was an integral part of the intense training for the rating. I can see the logic in it now, but at the time it was pretty ghastly. The other unanticipated trick came at about 5,000 feet. We were at cruise with the essence of cigarette drowning the innocents in the back seat; namely my brother Bruce and me.

Apache

Out of nowhere we took a very harsh dive downward; the kind where you're on a roller coaster at top speed racing toward the bottom. I couldn't believe I was going to have to live through it. I prayed and feared for my life at the same time. I held onto the red leather seat for my life and tried to let out a scream. It wouldn't come out; even though my mouth was open wide, I was breathless. My eyes bulged out as far as they had ever been allowed, and the trauma in the pit of my stomach was not to be forgotten. I thought the seat belt would tear through my back, as it crushed my ribs on the way. I was in serious pain, coupled with the worst fright I'd ever experienced in my life. I thought it would never end. I made up my mind right then and there that if I did make it out alive, my flying days were over.

After the lengthiest minute and a half, we pulled out of the dive which had turned into a partial spin. I didn't know which way was up, the disorientation was ever present and confusing.

With my last breath I yelled to the front, "What the hell was that?"

I got no answer, as if everything was within the course of normal and nothing unusual had occurred. I looked over to Bruce. I hadn't seen him in the past few minutes because I was so restrained that I couldn't even move my head sideways. He shot a look back at me as if to say, "They're out of their bloody minds, and so are we for coming with them." I knew that look anywhere, and I was in total agreement. Did they think that was fun? If that's what it takes to become a pilot, then you can count me out right now! We caught a break. They decided to land and take a breather. I understood the real meaning of the word; I was grateful, and committed to the notion of not going up again—ever! As with many bad experiences, one tends to forget or at least minimize them in relation to the present.

When I was tall enough to reach the rudder pedals, I really got the chance to get my feet wet and feel the thrill of piloting through blue skies, fog, and even an occasional thunderstorm. I steered away from the spins and the dives, making my fear quite clear. I endeavored to learn everything that this man could teach me, though I suspected I would neglect to get my pilot's ticket, even with all of those hours I would log. There is no doubt in my mind that though my father loved and lived his business, first in line after his family was his flying. It was an escape from life's pressures to a fantasy land where there was nothing between him and the heavens. He was at one with himself and the universe; there was an enduring calm interrupted only by the occasional squawk of the radios which signaled a potential weather problem, a marker, a warning, or aircraft within range. He was aware of everything around him; all of the engaging noises, any changing specks of light or dark in the surrounding skies, and yet he was totally withdrawn. Life on the topside was a mystical experience for him. There was something magical about the alluring interrelationship between the forces of this man and the airspace around him. We would fly for hours on end with nothing more than a few non-verbal communications; a change of the radio setting, a pointed finger in the direction of a passing aircraft, or simply an involuntary smile of expressed satisfaction. It was wonderful to share in my father's joy and to see him so totally immersed in something that gave him such saturated pleasure. It was like watching someone who's close to you when they open the present about which they've only dreamt, but never expected to receive. And so to know Pop was to fly with him, soaring to unparalleled emotional heights, experiencing a rare degree of closeness, and sharing the emotional contagion which surrounded him.

As I drove up to the hangar, the line crew had pulled the Aztec out, as I had requested. The sun was still pretty strong, so the reflection of the glittering metal was intense. As I turned in from the access road to the separate blacktop where all of the airplanes were chocked,

I could see that the Aztec had also been washed recently. She had been standing idle for several months now and really needed to be run up to maintain her mechanical ability. It wasn't good to let all of the oils and fluids stay still for too great a length of time. They would turn thick and possibly cause problems during the next flight. I had the choice of taking care of this myself or letting the airport crew do it for me. That of course was out of the question. I wasn't going to let anyone else take that pleasure away from me, and I certainly wasn't going to allow anyone but myself to get into this plane, let alone start her and taxi back and forth. I had an uneasy knotted sensation in my stomach. I hadn't been back here since before Pop had died, and the last time I had seen the Aztec was not a good one in my mind. It was at Bader Field in Atlantic City, just days before Pop left for Europe.

N6897Y "Yankee" Aztec

I unlocked the cabin door of the airplane with the little key which had been resting quietly in the desk drawer at the gallery. I had never used it; Pop always unlocked the door. I could still see him bending toward the door in his tan Levi's as he stood on the inside walkway of the wing, turning the tiny key to open the latch. "No Step" was prominently labeled near the flaps as a reminder. I was concerned that the weight of our bodies would dent or structurally damage the metal near the fuselage. The door opened with an inaudible click. I pushed gently on the handle which was slightly recessed to avert any extra drag and to maintain superior aerodynamic characteristics.

Pop and the Aztec

The smell of old leather was as encompassing as I had remembered. It had been locked up in there for months with nowhere to go, so it re-circulated and sweltered in its own divine fragrance as it matured. The tops of the seat backs were still ever so slightly shiny from the oils on the back of our necks, and they glistened in the late day sun which was weakening by the moment. I slipped into the left hand seat, straightened myself, and closed the door. As it shut, I could feel the pressure of the vacuum it sealed on the interior. My ear drums compressed, then relaxed.

I stared at the gauges in front of me, and as I did, the tears streamed down my face. Nothing was the same. There was a very distinct stillness within the cabin, which was devoid of energy and filled with lonely silence. This flying machine was in mourning for her friend who would return no more. My heart ached for her and for myself. We were a trio once, but we would never fly together again. Even if I were to go to ground school and get my private ticket, it would be too painful a reminder of the past.

I'd always been sentimental and had held onto pieces of the old days, but accompanying the airplane and her warm memories came the pounding remembrance of my father's death and its permanence. I cleared my eyes and cranked up the engines, left to right, and listened to their sweet purr which still had a mesmerizing effect on me. For a split second, I was next to Pop again and we were about to taxi down the runway when the shattering reality shook me....it was over. The noise of the engines returned and the seat next to me was empty. Damn it all, why did he have to die so soon? We had something so special; it was all history now.

I went through the procedural checklist and taxied out to the area where we used to run up the engines; away from the hangars where damage would result from the wake of the tremendous thrust. I ran them up to the maximum, one at a time, then together with my feet pressing hard on the brakes while the wings were buffeted by the wind of the twin Lycoming power plants. She began to buck and lurch with anticipation, as if her old master had returned once again, and for a split second I almost let her go, but I cut the power and returned to the hangar. The temptation to take-off was nagging, but without Pop it was meaningless. I knew my fascination with flying would never quit, but that I would also not pursue it; it was just too painful.

A tough step was in order, one which I knew was inevitable and which would grow more taxing as time went forward. I was going to have to sell the Aztec. Even if I were legally able to fly, it would be too distracting and too fraught with old haunts to keep her. It would be constant torture to continually fly with only half of the original crew, and though on one level I loved the idea. I felt it an unhealthy attempt to reach for something that wasn't there, and which would never be accessible.

Another problem confronted me, and that was the tight market for fuel-hungry twin-engine aircraft. We were smack in the midst of a serious energy crisis in late 1973, and it would be a grueling marketing challenge for me to get the sale consummated. Everybody was on a conservation bent, and here I was offering a gas guzzler for fun and recreation. I placed ads with a few top brokers whom I felt could get the job done. Surprisingly, it didn't take but a few weeks before we had serious interest and closed the sale. The saving grace which ultimately sold the plane was her pristine condition and youthful status. The motors had less than two hundred hours each, had just been through a "major" and there wasn't so much as a nick or paint chip to be found. Pop had provided her the best possible continuing maintenance, both mechanical and cosmetic. After all, this was his baby, and nothing was too good for anyone who was covered by the umbrella of his love! I was assured by the broker who represented me in the sale that his client would continue to provide the same loving care and concern for this airplane. He respected the sentiment the Aztec had come to represent. I suffered a tremendous degree of guilt and sadness in letting go of "6897 Yankee" as we knew her, but somewhere I was confident that my father would have endorsed my feelings of hardship if the situation were reversed, and would have done exactly the same thing.

Chapter Eight

Flying — Part II

I remember that cold Sunday in 1970 when my first left side pilot experience was scheduled. My many years of accrued flying skills would soon be put to the test. I bounded down the steps.

"See ya, Mom," I yelled over my shoulder.

"Good luck, Honey," she encouraged.

Pop was waiting for me in the car as I rushed out the front door and slammed it behind me. He sensed my apprehension.

"Nervous?"

"Yeah."

"You'll be fine; don't worry," He assured.

Twenty minutes later we were pulling into the lot at Atlantic Aviation—the general aviation facility at Philadelphia International Airport. The Aztec was shining with pride and awaiting my arrival. We zipped our ski jackets and stepped out of the car, hearing the echo of the thud of the closing car doors as we started my maiden voyage.

Pop and I walked around the airplane as we did the go-around, step by step.

"Okay, you know what to do. Pretend I'm not here," Pop ordered.

"No problem."

I checked for nicks in the propellers by running a gentle finger tip touch around the outer leading and aft edges of the blades. All was smooth and normal. There were no paint chips or dents in the wings on any of the surfaces. There was no stickiness in the rudders, ailerons, flaps, or fuselage. No oil leaks or fuel discharge or seepage from the engines. I opened the cowl flaps and inspected for frayed wires, thrown oil, cracked housings, chipped gears, and any other obvious disturbances. Next, were the pet cocks under each engine. They needed to be drained to eliminate any condensate that may have accumulated since the last start up. Any rust or incidental particulate would also be exhausted, as it was heavier than the fuel and would consequently drop to the bottom of the tanks to the drains. I examined the tires for tread wear, bald spots and under-inflation, all things not worth the risk of ignoring. No problems though; inflations looked good, lugs were tight and there were no apparent hydraulic problems.

"She looks good, Pop." I was satisfied.

"Let's go; time's getting short." He led the way.

We made it to the inside of the cabin. This time I got in first to take the controls on the left side. I was going to be the pilot. Pop was co-pilot. I was pretty confident until we got in and Pop said, "Okay, she's all yours....What's first?" I began to run through the regime.

"Adjust the seat so the rudder pedals are part of your feet. The brakes should be extensions of your toes since they're the top step of each rudder pedal. Seat belts fastened tightly, windshield un-obscured," I ran through the litany.

"From left to right when starting up," I had heard it hundreds of times as Pop would go through his routine. "Master switch on," I announced as I listened to the gyros spin with increasing volume as their whirring peaked."

Mixtures rich, pitches flat, throttles advanced enough to catch when fired up. Left engine always first, hit the starter, foot on the brakes, handbrake locked. A few quick cranks and she caught. A quick pull back on the throttle with the right hand so there's no over revving. Give her enough juice to idle smoothly and not cut out. Check the gauges; the tachometer, oil pressure, oil temperature, fuel levels, tank draw, alternator and engine temperature. They've all got to respond immediately and according to specifications.

"Looks good." I yelled over the drone of the left engine.

"Let's get number two up." Following procedure, the right hand engine cranked with ease and puffed the acknowledgment of a white smoke wisp ever so demurely and joined in idle with number one. The purr was deliciously synchronized after a few auditory adjustments.

"Ready?" Pop inquired.

"Nope," I replied, "not until the oil temperature needle is off the peg." Otherwise the oil is still gummy and might create a problem or demonstrate less than optimum performance. He smiled with confidence at my attention to detail and with pride at my success thus far. He had trained me well, though arduously I thought.

A few minutes later, the gauges were showing the go ahead mode. A quick twist of the wheel—left, then right—as I glanced out to the wings to watch their corresponding reflexes as the ailerons saluted accordingly. A pull of the wheel all the way back to my belly and then a smooth push forward indicated the working status of the rear quadrant. Strobe lights and wing markers on, call the tower for clearance. Ground control 121.7 I twisted the tiny knobs of the twin mark 12s, (two-way navigation radios), turned on the DME (distance measuring equipment), checked the glide slope, etc, and called ground control. I froze. I didn't remember what to say.

"Identify yourself," Pop reminded.

"This is Aztec six eight nine seven Yankee to ground control," I choked into the microphone.

"Aztec nine-seven Yankee, this is ground control."

Oh, my God. What do I say now? I took a chance with palms sweating and heart beating loudly. "Ground control, this is nine-seven Yankee for clearance to taxi to runway. We're headed to Atlantic City."

The response came too soon. "Nine-seven Yankee, you're clear to taxi runway twenty-seven, go 118.5, over."

"Niner seven Yankee out," I sighed gratefully.

I couldn't believe I'd made it that far. Down with the parking brake and off to the runway to hold short and rev the eager Lycomings up one at a time, then both together. Now I was ready, almost. I switched the radios to the tower frequency 118.5, but did all of the tests before making contact. The routine was fairly standard. Stand on the brakes; left engine first, throttled to 2,500 rpm and held there while scanning the gauges for appropriate responses. Check for feathering, drop in manifold pressure after magneto switching, electrical back up functioning, and bring her back down to idle. Now repeat it all with the right engine and then go through a brief parallel procedure with both engines together. Everything was looking good, time to get on with it.

"Philly tower, this is Aztec sixty-eight niner seven Yankee requesting clearance to taxi runway twenty-seven." I was feeling ever so confident.

The tower flashed the barometric pressure, wind speed in knots and direction, and then instructed, "Taxi runway twenty-seven and hold short."

"Niner Seven Yankee, over."

I re-calibrated the altimeter to comply with the updated information, released the handbrake and gently pushed the twin red throttle levers forward with my right hand while holding the wheel in my left and pushing on the right rudder pedal. We headed out to the airstrip being very careful not to get too close to the other aircraft that were chocked and tied down nearby. I enjoyed watching them wave and dip as the wake of our props let them know we were ready. I backed off and touched the brakes ever so slightly as we were rolling almost too fast. Their squeal was reassuringly comforting. I coasted out to the end of the taxiway and checked in with the tower as I approached the runway.

"Philly tower, six eight nine seven Yankee ready to go, runway twenty-seven, over." I declared.

Brief silence. Then, "Ninety-seven Yankee hold short twenty-seven, over," the tower ordered. I peered off to the left and there was the reason for the hold. A King Air was just coming down over the threshold. It would only be another minute before I'd be out there myself, getting ready to forward those throttle levers to their limit.

The air was crisp and dry, a typical January day. No clouds, just a brilliant metallic blue sky, but it was cold. The chill penetrated to the bone. It was one of those dry cold air days that hurt when I inhaled. I could feel that strange burning sensation as my lungs filled up; a good time to be inside where it was toasty; where all I smelled was the pungent permeation of the leather. The heat in the cabin had its own distinct flavor, a fragrance of the engine heat that emanated from the hot metals indicating that all was functioning according to design.

We were encapsulated in safe environs free from all other worlds. The sound of the air outside was thick, yet crackling with electricity. It echoed every noise of civilization, man's machines, trucks, and planes. There whistled the invisible wind that left its trace of momentary existence on the trees that waved and swayed with every passing gust, interrupted by the cry of an occasional passing bird whose journey to the south had been delayed or abandoned. The conspicuous tale of distant construction sounded the diesel clatter and pounding of earthmovers that repeated the destiny of the rivets being driven deeper and deeper into their metal homes. Inside the cabin there was none of that, only the occasional squawk of the radios and the squeak of the leather seats as we repositioned ourselves. The vibrations of the engines dominated all other auditions. They were the power that out-spoke any noise on the outside. All else was muted.

The King Air disappeared as it turned off the runway onto a distant taxiway.

A voice crackled, "Aztec nine seven Yankee cleared for takeoff on twenty-seven!"

The adrenalin began to surge through every vessel in my body. I was overcome with a flood of excitement. Even though Pop was next to me, he was silent with hands folded in his lap staring out the window. He was almost invisible. I was flying solo. I couldn't ask for his help as then it would not have been my own flight. I had to do this on my own. I was simultaneously reassured and petrified that he was next to me but only as a passenger. This was the real thing; I was going to solo a twin-engine aircraft. I'd done it so many times before, but not left side. Now all of the responsibility was on me. I could not screw up.

"Ninety-seven Yankee taking off, over," I replied with authority.

I hung up the mike quickly and gripped the wheel with my left hand and the throttles with my right. I cleared my throat, sat up straight, took a deep breath, swallowed hard, and pushed the red-tipped power plungers smoothly home in one steady forward motion as far as they would go and held them there. The roar was deafening. We started to roll instantly. The surge of power was absolutely frightening and dwarfed any I'd ever known. I felt my eardrums shudder, my teeth vibrate, and my face blur with the brute force of the thrust. I was pinned back into the seat by the massive horsepower pulling in the other direction. It was a battle keeping the plane on the ground. The tendency was for her to lift up and become airborne but we weren't at sufficient ground speed. The steering came mostly from the rudder at this point, but at seventy miles per hour, the ailerons were exerting their own force. The greatest challenge was keeping her dead straight on the center yellow line, for even the slightest touch on one of the rudder pedals created a swift deviation that required an equally delicate compensative push on the other to get back on course. The sense of unadulterated raw power was intoxicating.

We were charging down the black asphalt tire-stained straightaway with what felt like rocket speed with the white broken center line morphing solid as we gulped up more and more concrete. On the surface, it appeared that I was in total control but somewhere I knew full well that I was at the mercy of this magnificent machine— its designers and its builders were now calling the shots. It has to be every pilot's split-second nightmare that something will go wrong and instead of gracefully lifting off the ground, they'll wind up amidst a fiery mass of mangled, charred metal at the end of the runway with indistinguishable pieces and remnants strewn everywhere. Perish the thought! I looked down at the gauges to verify we were ready for pushback. The ground speed was eighty miles per hour plus and the runway was rapidly growing shorter. Time to take her up... right.... now!

"Push back...and...rotation," I declared.

I pulled back on the wheel just enough to lift the nose and

graciously got the main gear off the ground, leveling off slightly to earn some more airspeed. We were approaching 120 mph so I gave an upward pull and climbed steeply unable to see anything but topside. I slipped the safety latch off the landing gear lever and pulled it up. The sound was hydraulic like liquid squishing under pressure. After a few seconds the triple green lights blinked off indicating the wheels were properly tucked away. Now we could boost the airspeed without the risk of damaging the landing mechanism. Still climbing strongly, I turned out of the pattern and then backed off to cruise on the throttles. I leveled to a more modest ascent and thinned the fuel mixtures while adjusting the propeller pitches and trimming the nose to a more suitable level flight. Suddenly, it was noticeably quieter. The air was thinner and there was the recognizable rushing sound of the air as it passed by at 220 mph. Odd, I pondered, how you can't see it but you know it's there. It feels like you are going so fast as the earth moves by rapidly underneath you. The sensation of speed eludes you once you've left the ground.

I leveled off at 5,000 feet and relaxed for a minute, proud of my work thus far. I cooled my sweaty palms with the air swiftly pouring from a vent. Pop was smiling and reached over to give me a pat on the head, which turned into a squeeze of love, pride, and warmth. God, how I loved him! He was more than everything you could want in a father. He was the ultimate friend. How many guys my age would ever have the chance to ride in a twin-engine aircraft, let alone fly one? Here I was, hundreds of hours later at the controls of a Piper Aztec with nothing short of encouragement and inspiration to guide me through the vast expanse of cloudless skies.

I was pleased that the weather was good. I didn't need to complicate matters with having to file IFR (instrument flight regulations). There was enough to be done without staying on a predetermined course or following a series of vectors barked by one control center, and then another as we are handed off when entering a new territory. Having been through crappy weather many times before was anxiety producing enough.

I remember times when the weather wasn't as clear. There is a terribly confining feeling when you are totally IFR and visibility is zero. You can't even see the wings or engines. A sense of claustrophobia typically sets in and everything seems to swim around you as perception goes awry after an hour of this blindness. When the gauges are all you've got, you pray for a break in the soup, if only for an instant so you can re-orient yourself. *When will it end? It can't go on forever....or can it?* At 200-plus miles per hour, it was inevitable that we would eventually pull out to the fringe of the enveloping mass of icy gray moisture, but it could drift on interminably deteriorating by the minute. However, conditions often degraded with the impending threat of thunderstorms in the area.

On one such occasion, our fuel levels were dwindling and the ride was sufficiently turbulent that what began as discomfort grew into full-blown anxiety. There was no choice but to continue on and hope desperately that the clouds would break soon. I never enjoyed being slave to those stiff gusts of wind that shove the pit of my stomach into my groin and push my throat to my chin. That particular day, we were experiencing a continuum of bumps that distorted our hearing for an untimely second as our seat belts cut into our bellies. Our feet would simultaneously leave the floor while our heads abruptly greeted the ceiling. *We're going to die,* I thought. The not-so-distant purplish images of lightning reflected in the sightless landscape outside our cabin. Thunder resounded and rumbled tauntingly with a fierceness that rocked the plane as it resonated through our bodies and souls. *Why did I ever want to fly? Never again* I say to myself. *This is torture. Just get me through it this one time, I pray to you, God, and I'll do anything you ask; I promise.*

And so it went until the clouds graciously thinned out and blue sky gently slipped in. The fear always shows its ugly face when we are in the situation, but confidence gained through experience enhances the practice of stability. During the crisis, I think *it'll be a long time before I do that again*, but those moments of desperation and dread faded swiftly by the next time. Having survived my first audition, I would get through it again, and again, and again.

Nonetheless, I didn't have to submit to such conditions today. The elements would not mar my first solo experience.

After an uneventful flight in clear air on this crisp winter's day, it was time to come down. Atlantic City was discernible on the horizon. The ocean was visible only by the distant grey glitter of its un-polarized reflection. The texture was different from the land that bore a flat, tan look of stillness as opposed to the shimmering fluidic nature of the water. I began to prepare for our decent by pulling back on the throttles, making the mixtures rich and flattening the prop pitches. The altitude slowly dropped as I bled off airspeed. I trimmed the nose up by ratcheting the tab crank clockwise a few times. We were still going too fast to lower the landing gear and were still too far out to lose any more altitude. I spotted the airport, which I knew had no official tower so there would be no radio transmission. At least the runway was concrete instead of a grass strip that could rattle our teeth loose. I'd done that plenty of times at the backyard airstrips.

I went out past the airport over the ocean on the downwind leg. It was helpful but not all that essential. I could have slipped in after making a 180-degree turn at the shoreline, but I couldn't resist. It felt too easy; I was adventurous. I took flight over the blue-grey water and didn't look back. There was a genuine sense of being at one with nature. There was no other traffic, just the glare of the Atlantic below. Our tanks were fat enough to take us out an hour or so but I wasn't feeling quite that brave. After about ten delicious minutes of tranquilizing cruise, I gently bent her around casting a sweet farewell to my private frontier. I knew that someday I would return.

I could see the shoreline racing toward me from the horizon. The tallest buildings were becoming more prominent with each second as they grew in scale and identity. Soon, the lone winter stragglers walking the boardwalk would become animated as the long, thin, brown line would identify itself as we approached the end of the beach. Passing over the President Hotel was peculiar. This vantage point made it look skinny and small and not as grand as she appeared from the boardwalk. Only the black-topped roof with the brick perimeter was visible. The giant red letters that spelled out her name were so life-like. I knew we wouldn't hit them, but it was tempting to come in as close as we could without touching them.

I pushed down on the lever lowering the landing gear and listened for that familiar squishing sound as the hydraulic fluids and air pressures cooperated and lowered the wheels into position and locked them. There were the green lights, one...two...three.

"We're all set." I announced. I had a visual on the airport. We were beginning our final approach. Traffic had to be watched by eye for lack of a tower. And, there was plenty of it. It seemed as though everyone was flying into this airport today, singles and twins alike. Now, the challenge was to find our slot and get down fast. "Looks like we're next," I prepared Pop.

I twisted the wheel to the left and stood hard on the right rudder, creating a slip—a maneuver I'd watched Pop do many times. It caused a swift loss of altitude and speed. I was coming in hot and still too high; 140 knots and 1,000 feet. The sudden drop created the feeling of an elevator dropping and going sideways simultaneously. The blood drained from my face and at that particular point I was grateful that my stomach was empty. Thirty more seconds of strategic maneuvering and we held at 300 feet and 120 knots. The concrete was approaching like a moving train, rising up as we sank lower. I could see the double-yellow center line clearly. The throttles were in the vise-like grip of my right hand. Mixtures rich and pitch levers were positioned forward in case we had to make a missed approach and go up and around again. The green indicator lights still showed in triplicate on the landing stalk. Flaps were down two degrees to help us float in with the slight crosswind into which I banked the right wing slightly to stay on center. The nose dipped slightly. We crossed the threshold where I leveled off about fifteen feet above the runway to stay centered and then eased off the throttles. I pulled back on the wheel to lift the nose ever so slightly and flare as we settled gracefully down to business. Barely audible was the slight screech of the tires on the main gear as we touched. Once the main gear was down, I pushed forward on the wheel to sit the nose wheel on the ground, and at the same time exerted pressure on the rudder pedals to stay on center as we were rolling in at about eighty miles per hour. I gave a gentle nudge to the brakes and gradually slowed to a coast and turned off the runway to the taxiway. Idling over to the parking area near the two-room building, we could feel the breeze buffeting the wings as we turned perpendicular to it. I checked the gauges, held hard on the brakes, engaged the parking brake, and leaned out both engines at the same time. They slowed and choked to a sputtering halt. From right to left this time, all power off: electronics, avionics, and then the master.

The gyros continued their downward spiral and would remain noisy for several minutes. We unfastened our seat belts. Pop unlatched the door that was on the passenger side, and out we climbed. We were careful not to step on the wing or aileron surfaces. Only the narrow black sandpaper path was designed for safe walking. I locked up, put the key in my pocket, and jumped down.

Pop turned to me with a broad smile beaming and said, "That was great. I'm real proud of you, Buster." He put his arms around me and pushed his nose to mine and crossed his eyes with a clown-like gesture. I hugged him and said, "Thanks, for the experience and for the vote of confidence."

I chocked the wheels with the three large, yellow, worn wooden triangular log blocks so that a stiff gust of neighborly prop blast wouldn't bully our Aztec.

We walked over to the food shack. After a cup of the legendary machine coffee and a couple of packs of peanut butter crackers, we paid a visit to the water closet and went back to the plane.

I went through procedures and headed down the runway full throttle feeling the thrill of power and thrust as I pulled back on the wheel to head home. The winds had shifted a bit so the flight home was quickened at a cruise of well over 200 knots. It felt more like we were in a small jet because the "whoosh" of the air rushing by us was higher pitched than it was on our way to the shore.

We were approaching Philadelphia International Airport so I began my descent. I contacted the tower to let them know we were looking to get down and awaited a response. Traffic was light so we were cleared to land right away on runway twenty-seven. The gear was down, triple green light showing, nose trimmed, flaps up, mixtures rich, pitches flat....here we go.... I had plenty of time.

The concrete was long and wide. It stretched as far as the eye could see. I passed over the giant number 27 painted at the threshold and glided down to the ground. I kept the nose wheel off the ground until it just settled down by its own inability to stay aloft anymore. We zipped past the first cutoff and quickly coasted to the next one. I called the tower frantically because there was a DC-9 closing in behind me. There was no time to waste. Hesitation would prove disastrous.

"Aztec niner-seven Yankee clear to taxi off runway twenty-seven. Take next turn. Go ground control 121.7, over," the tower guided.

"Aztec, nine seven Yankee," I acknowledged, turning the tiny radio knob to the ground control frequency.

I throttled forward with a roar to clear the runway and watched as the red and silver DC-9 screamed past me on the runway and thundered to a thrust-reversing halt. I quivered as the vibrations passed through my spine, and paled at the thought of having delayed on the runway for even one more minute.

"Philly Ground, this is Aztec six eight niner seven Yankee requesting clearance to taxi to hangar, over," I miked.

"Aztec ninety-seven Yankee, this is ground control. Clear to taxi to hangar, over."

"Ninety-seven Yankee out," I finished.

I pulled to the front of our hangar, turned her around, and faced out so the ground crew could top the tanks with one hundred octane fuel and push the Aztec back into the hangar. I did one last gauge check and shut her down. Pop and I had invented a game to see if we could get the propellers to stop in exactly the same direction. A matter of aesthetics, it was purely at the whim of luck. This time the lady was in my favor. They stopped dead parallel on a diagonal. I looked at Pop and smiled at the perfection. He muttered with loving sarcasm, "Luck, that's all!" We both smiled and laughed.

Chapter Nine

Atlantic City

⤳ ⤳

The summer after Pop passed, Arlyn and I decided to drive to Atlantic City Shore. The drive to the shore was by anyone else's measure uneventful, but for me it was disquieting. The normal time from point to point would be a scant sixty minutes on the Atlantic City expressway where the speed limit was 70 mph. Of course, that meant 75 mph without question so the miles peeled off almost before they could be counted. It was Friday afternoon, close to six o' clock, and traffic was solid, but flowing smoothly. Everybody must have had the same idea to leave for the shore right after work. We were no different, sometimes stopping for Chinese food just before the bridge in Chinatown so we would miss the bulk of the traffic. By seven or so, it was not crowded anymore. The summers were built for the shore, especially on the weekends; a nice place to unwind after a hectic week in the dirty, hot, and congested condensation of concrete, asphalt, and brick. Adjacent to the ocean was the boardwalk which was a soothing place to walk until the wee hours of the night as the planks echoed with the cacophony of footsteps. There were always hordes of people walking as if to arrive somewhere when in actuality they just went from end to end in an aimless search for friends who were also there. There were amusement rides and arcades where one could challenge the odds for the chance of winning a stuffed animal to take home. The guys loved to show how skilled they were and impress their girlfriends with the spoils. Most of the time however, it was more frustration than luck, and the only thing they came home with was several dollars less than they had before their egos guided them to the challenge.

The atmosphere was carnival-like. There was cotton candy, flashing lights, circus-like shows, an abundance of noise, and of course the blended wafting essences of grilled meats, popped corn, roasting peanuts interspersed with stale cigarette smoke, and enough low life to satisfy even the most curious of onlookers. The piers definitely didn't draw the most luxurious element of people, but then again time spent there was minimal. The regulars who frequented the place belonged there, and likely felt right at home among the seamy vendors of chance. Farther up on the boards though, the air smelled less the commercial, and more of the sea. The people still dressed in contemporary attire rather than in the ripped shorts and crummy tee shirts of a couple of miles away. Uptown there was at least a partial air of respectability and everyone congregated peacefully recounting life in the city, or what had happened on the boat that day, or what the plans were for the balance of the summer. The older folk sat in the wicker stroller cars in front of the Ritz or the President, or the Ambassador, as they donned themselves in clothes that reeked of Miami Beach. The white jackets and complimentary colored slacks with the open shirts and patent slip-on shoes were the uniform of age. The whiff of cheap cigar smoke was standard as we walked by their corner. There was the constant requisite clatter of reminiscences of the days and years of a dimming past. Their generation had lived many years and somehow never made the transition into a more welcoming future. Those who'd made it financially drove the big and often grotesque Cadillac, while their wives donned the pretentious full length fur coats. Others were satisfied with boldly patterned sport coats and hats left over from the styles of the 40s and 50s. It was a classic sight, a microcosm in time that would forever retain its place.

Chelsea was the place for the "in crowd" to hang out. You could find everything from the teenybopper to the college set in that corner. Sometimes it was so crowded with such a virtual impasse that it took the police in their squad cars, driving right up on the boardwalk, to thin the crowd. It seemed like the police were a regular activity in front of Hi Hat Joe's, the fast food nook which had the pinball machines and greasy food all in one place. Be it day or night, the place was teeming with kids who were fairly well behaved but typically obnoxious as was to be expected for their age group.

That was the shore as we knew it in the 1960s, but for me it had taken on a different perspective. A year had passed since Pop's death, but it was still very fresh in my mind. As we were driving toward the shore, it seemed like we were floating above the traffic rather than driving with it. The line of cars was solid as usual, and we were moving at a brisk pace. There was an unusual quality of stillness in the air. I was driving with the windows open for a change. It was cool and it felt good not to have the artificial arctic atmosphere of the air conditioner and confined compression of closed windows. I was feeling slightly claustrophobic and began to retreat into a grey area of consciousness as we got closer to Atlantic City.

I tried to ignore the waves of pain and loneliness as we approached Bader Field, but failed to distance these persistent stimuli regardless of my efforts. I hadn't been back to the field since I sold the Aztec. The air field was coming up on the left in just a few seconds, and I would be remembering all too vividly how this was the last place I saw my father. I hoped against hope that I would make the light at that intersection, but predictably, there was no way. It changed to red just before I got there. At first, I stiffened and refused to peer off to the distance on my left side, but something made me turn and look. The tears shuttled down my face as I glanced over to the runway with the airplanes chocked neatly in order. The damned traffic light stayed red for an eternity and forced me to relive my horror. I had no choice but to remove the blinders and plow head on into the past, present, and future all at once.

I stared out at the sky above the field where once I'd watched the Aztec carry my father away from life. The wrenching feeling of separation was still so impossible to accept. It seemed so contemporary, so unwilling to be settled. I supposed then that someday it would get easier, but I knew that it was going take a lot of years. As I looked out to the field, I could still see Pop and myself walking back to the airplane entwined arm in arm as he explained his upcoming trip to Europe to me in detail. I felt the searing heat of the sun on my skin as we walked, the beads of perspiration on my brow, the intense warmth of our love which made everything all right with the world, and then I felt the sick knot in my stomach as I realized it to be over. The robust figure of that man in the tan Levi's nestled on his hips, wearing a short sleeve cotton button down shirt with the collar buttons undone, shadow on his face from the graying stubble, piercing blue eyes that danced with his zest for life, walking in his "space shoes" was indeed walking away. I could see him disappear into a visual haze before I had the chance to tell him that I loved him, just one last time. I was absolutely powerless to alter the course of history that was once the dawning future.

I continued to stare into space, looking for him when the horns of the impatient traffic awakened me to the light that had turned green again. Arlyn was silent and compassionate. She didn't speak or mention the light being green. She was fully aware of my every thought, and gave me all the space I needed to indulge my feelings. She also remembered those last moments with Pop, and had to suffer the indignities of his absence. The people in line behind us were eager to start their weekend; scurrying for parking spots where they wouldn't be towed away, standing in line in restaurants to consume the same old mediocre food, and then socializing while perspiring with the heavy salt air on the Boardwalk.

We drove on slowly traversing the crowds in front of us at the circle which was the main entrance to Atlantic City. I felt sad and bewildered after confronting the final and dismal departure grounds of that airport. It hurt again, but I lived through it. I knew that the next time would not be so fearful, though it would probably always be a standing monument to my final vision of Pop. I knew then that for all of eternity, as I passed that airport shrine I would always cast a wistful glance at what had once been a stack of beautiful memories.

A SPECIAL PLACE

We had dinner reservations for 8:30 that night. As we pulled up to the restaurant, Arlyn and I marveled at the elegance of the candlelight on the tables, and how delicate it made the floral arrangements appear through the street side windows. We parked the car nearly in front and walked in for a most expected experience of pampering elegance. It was the kind of place which was almost decadent in its richness and one that we saved for the best of clients or for the special times which would hold the fondest memories for the future. La Panetière was one of the most exquisite French restaurants in all of America. The Louis XVI décor was done to intoxication; the design pure French refinement. The offering of the evening was a whirlwind of French recipes which took three pages of menu in French to express. There were also masterworks of the chef that were not on the menu, but were available for the veteran patrons upon personal solicitation from the owner. It was a breathtaking evening in France for less than the usual one way fare; absolutely a divine experience to satisfy the soul.

Peter escorted us to our window table for two after extending his warmest salutations. Our friendship went back many years to the days when Peter first conceived the notion of such a magnificent re-creation. He had found this first floor space in the brownstone building on Locust Street at Sixteenth and imported everything from the simple fleur-de-lis wallpaper to the extensive French furnishings, Sterling flatware, French Crystal stemware, and his help, as well as all of the copper cooking utensils. He had once told me that his establishment would not only be the best, it would be the most expensive as well. It was all of those things and more. Truly a ceremony in saturation of only the most delicate of sauces which had been reduced for hours until mellowed to perfection, and which would be employed to marriage in combination with only the most supreme of ingredients involving either fowl, fish or beef. The game would be a selection of pheasant, duck, or hen, while the beef could involve either filet, lamb, liver or veal. The fish would be whatever was exotic or intensely rich. There were countless first courses of unparalleled delicacy, and divine desserts to nearly sicken all but the most inhuman of dwellers. The wine list read like an encyclopedia, with nothing but French vintage stock, though I must admit in later years the better California names made their appearance. The service was *parfait* and the courses were never rushed. When you dined at

La Panetière you did just that; it was an entire evening's experience. To reserve at 8 or 8:30, meant indulgence until at least midnight or slightly into the morning. It was far more than a meal of extraordinary perspective; it was an event of unique proportion.

Dinner had been extraordinary that evening. Everything was beyond perfect, but I began to feel a bit nostalgic. I neglected to realize that all of this richness brought with it the glaring absence of my father, with whom we had shared these pleasures in earlier years. Suddenly I began to feel unreal, a symptom of my running from a situation of feelings too intense for me to acknowledge. I would take on the quality of separation from reality, as if I were watching the whole scenario through a movie screen where I was on the other side looking inward. I could hear perfectly well, although the voices were distant, and I could see and respond to people as if they were right there, which they were, but it didn't feel as if they were real. I wanted to shake my head to make it go away, but it wouldn't work. The dream quality was unbearable and could only be penetrated by surrendering to my feelings, so I let the sadness filter into my waking dreams. Here we were in the midst of absolute splendor and I felt like I nearly ruined it.

I looked over to the table by the flower-filled fireplace, on which I had been focusing all during our dinner. I kept staring at that table, wondering why it was that there was a vacant seat. Ironically, the entire table was empty, but I only noticed the one unfilled chair. I then remembered with full impact that the chair was Pop's when we had all been there together...not so long ago. This was his place and I began to recollect all of the times we had enjoyed in the days of past. When I told him of Arlyn's election to the Honor Society at her college, he said, "God, that's wonderful! Let's celebrate; come into town and we'll go to La Panetière". We quickly got dressed and scooted into town for a rousing reception from Mom and Pop including Champagne and a feast of inordinate proportion. It was a totally spontaneous suggestion of insistence with an abundance of enthusiasm and love. This restaurant was reserved for very special occasions of celebration. There were so many, and so few, and now the tradition would continue on but without the major contributor who had been the founding member of the club.

Chapter Ten

New Beginnings

We put Mom to work in the business, gradually delegating her more and more responsibility. It was an unspoken entrapment of love to convince her of our need for her support and participation. We would, of course, be there for her. She knew that, but we all needed each other and we needed to convey to her the degree of our shattered condition. We felt it would give her a handle on life; an obligation to live and maybe, just maybe, a chance to someday laugh again. The situation was untouchably fragile, but she would manage ultimately to survive it.

At the same time, I had to get my own life back in order. I was so jolted by Pop's untimely death that I didn't know which way was up. I began to walk through life a step at a time carrying a brand new burden; a full-scale business which needed immediate attention and constant maintenance.

Our financial picture was plaguing to say the least. Pop had been involved in several very high cost deals into which he had invested some staggering sums of money. We had the goods as well as the plans for disposition, but we no longer had Sammy; our key man in the operation. The glaring question at hand was one of strained credibility. Would the clients with whom Pop had been dealing sit down and negotiate with us? Would they consider our corporation unable to fulfill the obligations which had been set upon us, or would they simply lose interest because they weren't dealing with the commander in chief anymore? There were several issues which now had to be addressed quickly.

Alan was certainly capable of handling the transactions, if the other players accepted him as a comparable replacement for Pop. Those were giant shoes to be filled, and none of us knew with any confidence to what degree we would succeed. We knew one thing: we had no choice but to cut the reins and go forward with every bit of muster we had in reserve. I owned only a few years of mostly indirect experience and was in a precarious position lodged somewhere between a rock and a hard place. I had always loved the business, but could rely on Pop and Alan to do the maneuvering while I learned and observed.

My demeanor at the time was not well suited for success; my hair was too long, my clothes too casual. Pop used to say, "You look like Ben Franklin; get a haircut!" It was more suggestion than request, but you can only push a kid in his early twenties so far when he thinks he knows it all, and when his long hair covers his ears preventing him from hearing properly. I thought it was cool to look like that. Everybody had long hair, thick pork chop sideburns, bell bottom pants. Dark conservative suits and well-groomed hair was for the older stuffed shirt generation. I proudly donned my American flag tie and flagrantly colored shirt of outrageous design.

In retrospect, I cringe from the memories of my appearance. Pop was quietly embarrassed at the sight of his unsightly child who made such foolish expressions in trying to prove himself. He must have been laughing hysterically inwardly as he viewed this absurdly tasteless fashion display which included shoes with outlandishly high heels and fabrics of slippery polyester. I didn't do drugs, even if I approximated the appearance of those misguided slobs who chose to space themselves out of the world. I had to quickly shift my appearance and attitude. There was absolutely no time to be wasted, my era of leisure had come to an abrupt and screeching halt. And so it began. I took Pop's place as an art dealer.

Our company was growing at a frenetic rate. The days of old were gone. We were determined to have continued success. We loved the odds and pushed through crisis after crisis, taking the bends smoothly at every turn. We were calling the shots, and our aggression grew commensurately with our skills. We were committed to expose all of the shadows of doubt with an expansive flood of light and continue the dream Pop had conceived for us so many years ago.

Alan and I worked marvelously well together, though our styles were markedly different in texture. He was much more intrigued in the scholarly aspect of the business; my heart was in the aggressive transacting end, so we worked out a remarkable blending of personalities. He would immerse himself in our research library of tens of thousands of volumes of art reference books and monographs we had amassed over the years as he searched for the solution to unsatisfied authorship, or for the latest market values of specific works of art. In the meantime, I would be closing the sales and hunting down more paintings for the gallery. We never felt any competition or feelings of superiority with each other. We were equals with nothing but admiration for one another and expressed only genuine wishes for our mutual success. We were a team born under the most dire of conditions. We ran the rocky road of new frontiers together and developed new bonds of closeness for which we continuously heard the utmost praise. It is, as we have seen and been told, most rare for fathers and sons and brothers, all in the same family business, to be the best of friends. For us it came naturally; it could not have been any other way. Our love for one another was too strong; impenetrable by outside stimulus. Some would have settled for less...we would not!

We enjoyed an extraordinary reputation which we continued to promote. Many of our clients were mutual, but we each retained a specific "his" or "mine" list, and respected each other's territory with the exception of an impending loss of an important sale due to the absence of one of us in the face of a surprise visit by our client. We both agreed vehemently never to forgive one another if we lost a sale on the account of deference to boundary. We knew how immensely proud Pop would've been, if he could have seen how well everything had worked out; how we remained the best of friends. It has to be a father's dream, his deepest wish, to have his children become as close as Alan and me. We only wished he were there to share it with us.

Chapter Eleven
How Arlyn and I Met

Arlyn and I had been married for less than one year when Pop died. Although she only knew him for a brief time, Arlyn adored and admired this saintly man. Pop loved her as a daughter and was happy for the both of us. Celebrating our first year anniversary brought back memories of how Arlyn and I met.

I graduated from Oglethorpe College in Atlanta in 1970 with a Bachelor of Art degree in business. It was time to come home and begin my new life. I fell into the family business without much hesitation and stayed with my parents in the house for about six months or so. I soon felt the need to get an apartment of my own. I could afford something half-decent so I began to look in the newspapers and in the telephone book. I really wanted to be in town and live in a high-rise building with good parking. It had to be safe, air-conditioned, and in a good location with adequate staff. The Windsor at 17th and the parkway in downtown Philadelphia seemed to have everything

I needed. It overlooked the parkway, had a small but full kitchen, a shower and a bath, a walk-in closet, and a substantial living area where I would locate my bed, stereo system, and television. There was even room for a chaise in the corner. The rent was within range and the parking was fair, so I made an appointment with the rental agent to take a look at an efficiency unit. I signed the lease and moved in shortly thereafter. It was really nice to have my own place.

I didn't receive the mailbox key the day I moved in so I went to the office the next day to ask for it. In the same breath, I said, "Who is the girl over there?" I motioned to the dark-haired beauty sitting at the typewriter in the inner office.

"Oh, you want to know about her too?" the lady smiled.

"Yes....yes, I do." *I hope she isn't married.*

"She's my niece. She is working as a rental agent this summer. Do you want to meet her?"

"Could I? That would be great!" My heart pounded out of control. I swallowed a suddenly dry throat as my tongue struggled to push the words out. Suddenly, I was as nervous as a cat and didn't know why. Had she called my bluff? Was I really interested, or just afraid she wouldn't be as interested in me as I was in her? I don't know what was going on but I went for it.

"Just a moment. I'll go and get her," she sweetened as she walked away. I watched as she bent over the girl's shoulder to whisper my request. She flashed a brief but penetrating look my way and then rose from her chair and came over to be introduced.

"Hi." I was charged with electricity as we met.

"Hi." She smiled cautiously.

"I just moved in to the building." Growing more courageous, I added, "Can you talk for a few minutes?"

"Sure, why not?" she relaxed. We stood outside the elevator talking for nearly an hour. "Call me sometime," she offered as she left to go home.

I gave her a quick kiss on the cheek. Holding her hand, I assured, "You will hear from me...very soon!" I would have been content to spend the rest of my life talking with her right there but our lives had to move forward.

I reluctantly caught the elevator upstairs to my new home. When I got to my apartment I felt dazed—like I'd been whacked over the head. I was spinning with excitement, my breathing was erratic, and my heart was fluttering with a wild wave I'd never felt in my life. I had taken a deep plunge head over heels in love. I could not function for the rest of the day, and nothing else mattered to me. Every time I thought about her, my heart raced frantically. And think about her I did, during every waking moment. I was positively out of control, obsessed with this incredibly beautiful girl who had just stepped in my life and taken my heart.

It didn't occur to me until the next day that I didn't get her phone number. A frantic search of all the Riebers in the telephone book proved futile. I would have to wait out the weekend and hope to see her Monday after work. That weekend may as well have been a month for it seemed never to pass. I counted the hours, the minutes, and even the seconds as they swept past the numerals on my watch. It was torture.

After work on Monday I raced home hoping she'd be there. Fortunately, she realized that she'd forgotten to tell me she lived with her grandparents whose name was different from that of her own. Knowing I would never find her in the phone book, she hung around on Monday until I got home.

"Oh, my God! Am I ever grateful to see you?" I wrapped her in my arms and held her as a new found treasure. "I was going out of my mind. I looked for you in every phone book and..." she covered my lips with hers.

"I know; I am so sorry. I should have given you my number. I just couldn't think straight after we met," she confided. Her breath was hot with passion as her eyes danced with desire. I tasted the sweetness of her kiss as our lips brushed with longing.

"I could not stop thinking about you all weekend."

"Same for me." This was so right, so delicious, so very perfect.

"Hey, I wish I could stay and chat, but I have to go to a funeral tonight for a gentleman who worked for us. I promise I will call you the second I get back. I shouldn't be late; I'm just going to pay my respects."

I quickly wrote her number in my checkbook and handed her a slip of paper with mine on it. We were on our way to a lifetime embraced in unison.

When I got home that night, we talked on the phone for hours. It was as if we'd known each other for years. It was heaven on earth for both of us. I knew then that we were meant to be together.

Arlyn and I were married eighteen months later on December 23, 1972. As of 2008, we have seen thirty-five wonderful years together. She is still the love of my life. I am so happy that I followed the urging of my inner voice to go out and find my own apartment that day. Some would say its coincidence or irony that I was looking for an apartment at the same time Arlyn happened to be working in the building for the summer. I know it was destiny and I am forever grateful.

Chapter Twelve

My Old House

My life had numbered two and a half decades. It had been many years since I had moved away from the old neighborhood called Mt. Airy, and it took a long time before I worked up the courage to venture back to visit. I would always devise a detour to avoid it if I happened to be nearby. My desire to see the old house was strong, but the fear of what it would dredge up paralyzed me. I had finally gotten to the point where I was fed up with the limits that my fears were setting for me, so late one sunny afternoon about a year or so after Pop's death, I went out of my way to satisfy the yearning to go back to my childhood home.

It took about thirty minutes to get there from town. I instantly recognized a lot of the old streets. I turned left onto Stenton Avenue from Washington Lane and remarked to myself at how the architecture of the neighborhood had worn down from abuse and lack of care and attention. I couldn't believe how small the streets looked. As a child on a bike they seemed so wide and everlasting; now they were dwarfed by time and perception. Duval Street was first, with my old bank on the corner. There it stood, the Liberty Savings Bank, flanked by a strip of indistinguishable neighborhood stores on the right, including a toy store, corner delicatessen, grocery, and small restaurant. Johnson Street was the next light, with the drug store on the other side of the street. I remembered going in to buy a half gallon of Breyer's chocolate ice cream for a dollar and a nickel. Funny how certain things stick with you. Next, was Barringer Street, then Cliveden Street onto which I turned right and coasted down the short hill to the next intersection at Mansfield Avenue. At the stop sign, I proceeded to cross as I gazed up the street to the fourth house on the left—number 1505. I cut the engine and drifted down the street as the car slowed to a gentle halt in front of my old house.

I smiled as I admired the beauty of what I had expected to have been run down through the years. It seemed like generations had passed since I had grown up there, but the house was still as beautiful as ever. The shutters were still painted carmine red, and the fieldstone of the structure was very much intact. The front porch maintained the white twin benches under the overhang, and the porch on the left side of the house was still as if it were in a southern mansion suspended by those four white pillars. The roof was thick, gray slate with those funny little sections of metal protruding upward to prevent sudden snow slides in the winter. The shrubs were lush green and in full bloom, while the pink azaleas exploded everywhere. They had grown to an enormous height, but were evenly trimmed and kept shapely. Even the grass was meticulously manicured; it had the look of a well-groomed golf course—no weeds in a uniform blend of the finest variety of lawn. The owners had obviously taken great pains to maintain the integrity of this house.

I was awarded the memories of the good times we had in this old neighborhood. The faces of the friends with whom I had stayed close through the years came to mind. The days of building go karts in the garage, riding the paratrooper motorbike in the driveway, trying most valiantly to get it started while running almost the entire length of the drive to get it to kick over. Some days it worked; some days it didn't. We had to pump the left tank with air and then the right one to force the fuel through the lines. It was basically a very primitive system, which was temperamental and not very sympathetic. I don't know how the paratroopers ever got them to work when they landed.

The driveway was a constant source of amusement. I spent many hours sitting in the baby blue 1964 Peugeot which was actually Mom's originally, then Bruce's, then finally mine. I consumed hours upon hours in the driver's seat practicing with the four-speed column shifter as I worked the clutch and the gas pedal as if I were competing in the Le Mans. Though I was still too young to drive, I learned how to manage it so I could drive anything when I took the test.

Beyond Bruce's room on the rear of the second floor was a sun porch, which was really a great place to catch a tan. I used to take out a thick towel, a radio, and a drink, and stretch out there for hours. The only problem was the bees which were plentiful because of all the nearby rose bushes on arched trellises that framed the rear perimeter of the house. The fragrance was divine, but the buzzing wasn't very soothing. Every direction yielded a splendid panorama of red, pink, orange, and yellow roses that climbed and turned and twisted their way to the top of the white-gated ladder with a gracefulness that only Mother Nature could display. Each had its own specific perfume as if the color would complement the scent. There was sweet and there was sweeter. It was a dreamscape.

There was the basement with a wet bar, which I used for my darkroom. It was perfect with sinks and everything I needed to develop all of my own 35 mm film in black and white, which I felt to be much more creative. I'm not sure whether it really was more creative, or because I wasn't prepared to work in color. I had my own enlarger, and I used the laundry room sinks to further the perfection of my product. I also used the basement to practice with my rock group. The acoustics were awful, but we sounded terrific anyhow. There was enough echo and reverberation that I don't think anyone could have sounded too bad. The place definitely held a large bank of fond memories.

I felt like such a big shot when Mom and Pop would go out for a late night on the town, and Alan and Bruce were away for the weekend. I had the whole house to myself. I could do whatever I wanted without any restrictions except for a few basic prohibitions. What I found to be most frightening were the bizarre noises that the house made when no one else was there. God, how it creaked and cracked and squeaked. It got worse as the night grew longer. It got so bad that once in a while I would go downstairs and yell in a bravado voice, "If anybody's down there, I'm gonna kill you. This is your chance to get out before we come after you!" I would act real tough. All the while, I was shivering in my boots. I'd gather all the courage I could borrow and open the door leading to the basement, and turn on the light while I talked super blood and guts. "Okay, you better not show your face! Nobody better mess with me, or it'll be the end of you." Then, I would slam the door with an attitude of arrogance and conviction. Nobody would venture forth after that unless they were really masochistic. Fortunately, no one ever responded due to the fact that there was never anyone there. But as a child, some very strange things go through your mind, and as you grow up, some of them stay with you. It all depends on the strength of the fears that lie beneath the distorted notions.

I awoke from my trip into history and thoroughly enjoyed my visit with the old house. It was very satisfying but was also a trifle disconcerting in that I no longer belonged there. The past was packaged as memories now, and some of the more delicate ones had already been shattered. As I thought of all the wonderful experiences we'd collected and enjoyed in those years, I was saddened that things could never be the same again. Suddenly, the house became just another configuration of architectural achievement as I tucked the images back into place where they felt comfortable.

I started the engine and shifted from park to drive. No longer able to hear the sweet lullaby of the neighboring birds, I headed back to the future. But not without one more glance into the mirror...

Chapter Thirteen

Winter Reminiscences

I awoke to a certain brightness in my bedroom—a brightness that could only mean a supernatural presence was making itself known or that it had snowed while I had been asleep. It was the latter. It was also the first snow since Pop had died and I wondered how his body might be fairing under the white winter blanket. It had been years since I'd seen snow this deep. That, of course, caused me to remember the times I had with him as a child when it snowed. My mind started sledding down memory lane as I stalled from getting out of bed...

Suddenly, it all seemed so familiar like I'd lived it a thousand times before. The snow was a fresh-fallen, pure, unspoiled powder. It looked as if there was an accumulation of two to three feet. No tracks, no plows—just a frozen, undisturbed field of silence with not a soul in sight. The wind was howling and gently shaping the landscape with dunes and drifts. The temperature must have been in the single digits carrying a deadly wind chill partner of forty below zero. Barely discernible were the white blanketed humps that indicated our cars in the driveway. This was Mother Nature's way of earning respect by putting modern technology into the basket and redefining man's inability to compete with a grander force that is ever present, omnipotent, mysterious, and evasive. We were diminished at her whim, but it wouldn't be long before another change would come about and we would counter it with minimal intelligence.

The next morning we would awake to the faint muffled sounds of the scraping of shovels somewhere nearby as the big metal scoops ground against the concrete to carve their paths through it. I jumped into my clothes, geared up for the bitter cold, and grabbed the shovel. The snow came up to the halfway mark on the storm door. To get out, I had to push the door open as far as it would go and squeeze my body through. I sank to my waist and felt cautiously for the steps that were down there somewhere.

As a child, it seemed like every winter saw at least six major storms. There was no satellite weather forecast, no sophisticated computer storm tracking equipment; just hard winter expectations. It was always great to see a big storm because it nearly went unsaid that the schools would close for a day, sometimes two. Winters were for fun, not for school. Winters were meant for sledding, building forts and having snowball fights, and sitting with family by log burning blazes in the fireplace. We could forget our normal daily rituals while we dealt with other situations like frostbite, frozen and soaking pants, and wet gloves.

After the plows had cleared the main cross street at the end of the block, they would leave tremendous piles of snow on both sides of the street. We had our big '62 Oldsmobile ready to go; snow tires and chains. Everybody had chains; we would all take our cars to the gas station on the eve of a big winter storm and they'd put them on for us. There weren't any horrible crowds because not many cars were around then. In fact, there didn't seem to be that many people either. We had to be careful driving after the chains were installed. They could break on dry ground and mark up the wheel cut-outs if they got a little too loose. The plows had cleared a one-lane path down the center of our street and we were ready for some fun. School was closed and Pop took the day off from work. While waiting for our car to warm up, we shoveled a path through the white four-foot barrier that blocked our car in the driveway.

"Let's go!" Pop yelled with impish excitement.

We jumped in the car and buckled our seat belts. Pop revved the engine a couple of times and turned onto the street. He took aim on the mountainous drift at the end of the street. With a running start, the snow crunched beneath the wheels as Pop drove faster and faster. Nothing could stop this gleaming silver, two-ton metal beast. The snow wouldn't dream of resisting our frivolity. Twenty miles an hour and charging toward the white-walled monster. Closing in.... ten feet.....six....two..Wham!! God, what a thud. It sounded like an avalanche. Snow flew explosively in all directions. The sky was powdered and we were hysterical with laughter. The success of our mission coupled with the ear-splitting roar of our breakthrough caused Pop and me to roll with uncontrollable laughter. It pleased us to see the residents of nearby houses come running out to see what the hell had just happened. The neighbors must have thought we were totally crazy. This would go on for hours, until we'd blown apart as many drifts as we could find. We thought it humorous that we could redesign the architecture and slop up the streets. Somebody had to unlock the white snow gate at the end of the road, or we'd all be locked in until it melted in the spring.

As dusk approached, the air got very still and grew colder with every breath. The early stars appeared faintly in the northern sky, twinkling rhythmically as they grew brighter against their darkening background. The moon cast a pale blue-white shimmer over everything as its fluorescent glow bathed stone, brick, and snow alike. How poetic nature could be. There was nothing more romantic; except maybe for the logs crackling and sputtering in the fireplace of the old house. We piled them on strategically to let the air flow freely, and then shove some crumpled sheets of newspaper under the andirons. The orange glow leapt quickly to a roaring superheated blaze. The heat was so intense that we couldn't get closer than six feet, even with the screen closed. It was like baking in the midday tropical sun. The heat gave our faces a tightness reminiscent of a Florida sunburn.

When the inferno in the fireplace settled to a bed of glowing orange embers that winked and faded with every change in the draft, we would get pieces of salami to skewer or roast, or apples to bake on a stick. Sometimes we tossed seeds from oranges and tangerines in the fire just to hear the gentle puff they emitted when they blew apart. It was inevitable that sleep would overcome even the most alert one of us. The heat would bathe us in serenity and force us into subtle drowsiness, which disappeared abruptly as the coals donned their ashen gray coat of exhaustion. Suddenly, the chill was back. Legs and feet grew cold. Faces stiffened as they were recaptured by the frigid downdraft slipping through the chimney. Time to go to bed. We secured the fireplace so no nasty surprises would ensue while we slept. Up to those icy winter sheets and air that had become chilled when the heat shut off, which it inevitably did because the thermostat was in the living room not too far from the fireplace. When we learned that the heat of the fireplace would prevent it from dropping low enough to force on the heater, we began to wrap the thermostat in aluminum foil to trick it into submission.

The next day Pop would take us sledding to the "Neckbreaker," the infamous tree-laden slope which had earned its name near Central High School. The safest end of the hill would provide a long, clean ride—not very exciting, but perfect for small children and the "easy to pale" folks. The thrill ride was a forty-five-degree slope at the opposite end. That in itself would have been adequate, but there were hidden moguls when traversed at high speeds would suddenly make us airborne with a wrenching upward motion that would render us awkwardly helpless for a couple of frighteningly unpredictable seconds. If we were skillful, and a trifle lucky, we maneuvered to a safe, albeit sloppy, and hard landing. If we weren't coordinated, we rolled off in midair, or worse, got tossed as our sled hit the ground. It was a real riot to watch as long as we didn't get slammed into a swiftly passing tree when not paying attention to our own ride. If we survived a run, we were cheered with congratulatory support, and challenged to do it again.

Alan, Bruce, and I had been there many times in previous winters, but upon Pop's first experience we told him that it really wasn't as bad as its reputation.

"Try the Neckbreaker," I told him. "It's not that scary. It's more hype than fact."

Pop was unsuspecting and didn't think much of it. He watched a few brave souls test it out and walk away jubilant and raring for more.

"Alright," he owned up to the dare. "I'll give it a try."

Pop laid down on his belly with his feet extended over the rear of the sled. We lined him up and gave him a gentle shove while we giggled amongst ourselves. Down he went at a blinding pace with a spray of white dust trailing from his runners. The mogul lurked but a few yards ahead. He zoomed into it with ever quickening momentum as we watched the speeding missile launch itself almost three feet into the air.

"Record height!" we laughed hysterically.

"Oh, no!"

He was flying off the sled; something was wrong! We tore down the hill after him. He was motionless as he lay face down in the snow.

"Oh God, we killed him," I scolded. "How could we have been so stupid?"

We got to Pop and slid in next to him. His eyes were open.

"Are you okay, Pop?"

"Yeah, thank God! I'm just winded and a little stunned after what you guys put me through."

"I am so sorry, Pop. We were just messing around," I explained. "I didn't mean anything by it. It was stupid. I'm really sorry. Are you sure you're okay?" I had withheld information, and by doing so, jeopardized his safety.

I'm okay." He put his arm around me. "Don't worry about it." Pop forgave us but I never forgave myself.

"I'll never do anything like that again."

I refused to sled anymore that day.

Chapter Fourteen

A Portrait of Pop

With each day, wearing Pop's shoes grew more and more uncomfortable. In retrospect, I think they must have been rather ill-fitted to my feet. Perhaps it was just the dawning recognition that I wasn't my father and that he wasn't me. I was astutely aware that I was grasping at pieces and fragments of my past trying to hold on to him, but it wasn't working anymore. I walked around enveloped in a haze of annoyance. I was surrendering my own identity to a man whom I had loved and would continue to love even in his absence, but I surely wasn't about to disavow myself for anyone; dead or alive.

I began to look upon those wine-colored slippers with growing disdain! They were conspicuously out of place on my feet—out of context, anachronistic. They belonged to another place in time. I was compelled by the feeling that my independence was being shoved into retrograde. I could no longer tolerate growing old so quickly. Pop's feet were taking control of my mind as well as my body. I had to assert myself or be forever absorbed by this ever-dominating force. I did with dignity the only thing that was left to do. I threw the ragged pair of leather soldiers into the trash. They had served me well, but it was time to walk forward again and understand that glances backward were sufficient. There was no longer a need to return for more than a brief visit.

It wasn't that I didn't want to be or look like Pop. He was genuinely handsome. His steel blue eyes burned brightly as they wielded power and sensitivity. His face was characteristically successful with tenderness and charm, and yet it read with the ease of a child's storybook. When he spoke, his eyes danced with delight and sparkled with evocative luster. Those windows to his soul revealed the deep feelings of compassion for those who earned them. When you looked at him you would see a man of unending tenderness who exuded such warmth that even a stranger would be a stranger for only a moment. Those piercing blue lights welcomed and beckoned trust while giving assurance of friendship and a guarantee of sincerity. He asked nothing in return but sincerity. The magnetism of his charisma was too inviting and too innocent to resist.

If his eye contact didn't attract you, then it would be the tenor of his voice, the music of his speech, or his positive energy. One would be losing something incredible if they missed an opportunity to be around him. Every day was an experience which could only be countered by the next. It wasn't that there was always something so exciting to outdo the previous episode, but rather it was the exceptional quality of each second spent with him. Even the most mundane of tasks was performed without boredom. Life was truly an adventure when played by the hand of Sam David.

When he passed, Pop's hair was graying and was swept back with remnants of childhood blond. I had seen pictures Mom carried in her wallet from the time when they were dating. Those pictures showed a young and handsome man with an unsettled look about him. His fashion was gangster-like. A cigarette dangled from the corner of his mouth as the wisp of smoke drifted past his face. His glare was one to revere and respect. The photograph was black and white, but told the tale of this young man's destiny in full color. As he aged, his hair thinned and then finally abandoned him, leaving the sides intact and something more than just memories along the top of his head. He grew more and more handsome through the years, though he never accepted the white beard that he raised for a few weeks growth. The vision he saw was an intrusion on the illusions of his youthful image that seemed to be escaping his grip. He wasn't ready to face the likes of Ernest Hemingway in the mirror, so he quietly and abruptly erased it with his electric razor and restored the radiance which still lurked underneath the mossy masquerade.

Blue was Pop's color. He looked fabulous in navy slacks, a powder blue shirt and sky blue sweater. He really didn't expend any extra effort to be a true fashion buff, but he never appeared less than dapper. His taste in clothing was as delicate and elegant as was his style in life, so it came naturally that he dressed to the nines. He knew how to dress for every occasion; appropriately. His clothing bowed toward the conservative side, with a wardrobe of dark blue and gray business suits. Occasionally, he would vary the theme with a blazer and pair of slacks, but one that would be accepted among a wide range of clients. His ultraconservative ties were a combination of club, paisley, and stripe; the majority being of a dark background with a subtle burgundy or reddish pattern. Jewelry was never his way, so there were no rings to be seen on his hands. A small 14-karat gold tie clip in the shape of an airplane was the limit and his trademark.

The other side of life for him was broached with tan Levis and short-sleeved shirts, and if it were sufficiently cold, a lumber jacket.

The last one he had gotten as a present from Mom was a dark brown leather bomber waist jacket. He loved the way it felt on him and the way he felt in it. It was the jacket of an ace pilot, and he fit the role perfectly. Pop was a regular guy totally unaffected by his peers and his own successes in life. He knew his worth, but never abused it by stepping on or judging anyone who had less. If anything, he would feel sorry for those who were less fortunate.

His appearance was very impressive. He was a substantial five feet eight inches, carrying a well-proportioned 175 pounds sporting an athletic structure of wide shoulders, a broad barrel-shaped chest, no hips, and thin tapering legs. His pants invariably hung too low because of his hipless waist. I can see him as he pulled his pants up with both hands after even the briefest walk. He made no attempt to cover this flaw in his build; it was him, pure and simple.

His shoes were generally imported and expensive, and probably uncomfortable, or so they appeared. Colors were again reasonable and fell within the confines of the acceptable black or burgundy for business. The others were for fun and consisted of a mélange of boat shoes, tennis shoes, and space shoes—a creation designed to be an exact fitted mold of the foot. They were the most grotesque looking things imaginable as they approximated an upside down barge with veins running the length of the shoe. Though I could never bring myself to wear something so ugly, they were reputed to have been the most exquisitely comfortable footwear ever created.

In his later years, Pop developed crow's feet that were especially noticeable when he was suntanned as they spidered around the outer perimeter of his eyes. They were probably a result of squinting as he confronted the solar force while flying his airplanes or while enjoying the ocean expanses aboard the various yachts of his friends and clients. Most people dread the look of such telltale wrinkles, but they only enhanced his rugged face. His face and scalp would turn a vibrant shade of bronze, his hair lightening to a more golden color of blond, making his blue eyes shimmer in glowing contrast.

The face would generally serve as a barometer of his well being. If there were considerable pressures weighing upon him, he'd lean out and look slightly gaunt or peaked. If things were going on an even keel and his nerves were in a state of calm, he would eat a bit too heavily and his face would round to greater fullness; not fat, but enough to lose a fraction of facial definition, and induce the hinting possibility of another chin. Most times he was on the run and entertaining with rich food for the sake of his clients who enjoyed the luxurious pampering when making a substantial purchase. For a while, the saturation is delicious, but it doesn't take very long for it to become a sacrifice rather than a pleasure. The richness can be a killer and the evidence mounts quickly with the additional weight that refuses to leave without an extraordinary measure of effort and willpower.

His muscular build was astonishing! He had the biceps of a teenage weight-lifter and the chest and shoulders of a football player. We used to arm wrestle and he would put me away. I always envied his power, but found security in the same force that had just precipitated my defeat. He was tough, with legs of immeasurable strength and feet that propelled him at an almost unethical speed for a man of his age. Where did all his energy come from?

His hands alone could bend metal and be at the same time so gentle as to comfort a crying infant. His skin was as soft as silk, except for the gruff whiskers on his face. My skin would peel off sometimes as his razor-like half day growth would sand my face as it brushed me with his kiss. It was worth the scrape though, for his affection was without doubt one of the most comforting and soothing elements in my life.

As I grew older, I found myself developing the very same kind of body and muscle tone. It was a thrill to be like him, but there was an uneasy sense of equality. I was overcome with happiness and joy, but sadness encroached upon the good feelings when it struck me that I was now as strong as my protector. I would soon supersede his strength. He was getting older, and though he was tough, and far wiser, it was evident that I was now blossoming with the same youthful force as the master's. I became the protector, which to him was both a source of tremendous excitement and unforgiving self-appraisal. He watched with pride as I grew and ached my way to manhood, hoping that I would develop far beyond his own limits. A flood of satisfaction filled his heart when I arrived at a point in life where I could sustain myself and a family as I stretched to new levels of achievement. He never fell victim to such complex emotional conflict in watching me succeed, but there had to have been a feeling of taking second place as he dropped behind with slightly slower stride.

There was one final obstacle I had to overthrow. I had been using Pop's briefcase for nearly a year after his death. If that weren't enough, it still had his initials on it. At first, I felt honored to walk around with his case and his initials on it. It must have been my method for retaining his style and his image. I finally had the small monogram changed from SD to CD. The Italian leather case itself was very handsome. It was thin and black with two small gold latches on either side of the handle. It didn't hold very much, which made it quite impractical, but it was sharp looking from any angle. It was also pretty heavy, but I didn't care; I could carry a tremendous amount of weight...or burden.

At last, the novelty had worn off. I awoke to the realization that I was demonstrating varying degrees of irrational behavior. I was not living in the present, I was caught in a profusion of history. I could no longer keep up the charade. The shoes and the briefcase were sentimental and protective. They posed as a link to my father, automatically providing a cover for my own fears and insecurities as they arose after his death. These items rode shotgun while I stumbled back to my feet. They assisted in fending off the villains of my imagination until I could reach the point where I was stable enough to trust my own instincts. New experiences had always proven difficult; I was grateful for the exterior adornments.

Chapter Fifteen

The Birth of a Son

One of the greatest joys life has to offer is the birth of a child. In the spring of 1976, Shawn, our eldest son, was born. Once he made his way to daylight, he rested on Arlyn for a few minutes. When I held him in my arms, every emotion I'd ever known flooded through my very essence and overwhelmed me. I was holding a living, breathing being that we created nine months ago when we decided we were ready to grow our love into a family. My face was salty with a tearful mixture of joy and sorrow; it was a bittersweet time. A new life was ours to cherish and develop with the best parenting skills we would bring to the table. And yet, there was a tremendous gap, something so amiss that I could feel the choking thickness of the vacuum. A glaring sadness enveloped me and I awakened to the stark reality that Pop would never hold his grandson. He wouldn't be there to take him to play ball, build a go kart, vacation with him, baby sit, watch him take his first steps, or take him flying to share the wondrous moments of solitude above the earth. All of those special things in life that memories are made from.

"I have a son!" I telephoned my mom soon after Shawn was born. The joyous delight I felt was tinged with so much emotion that could barely get the words out.

Later that morning when Mom got to the hospital, we walked together to the baby viewing area. There were dozens of new lives in little plexiglass cribs, wrapped with blankets, and identified with name cards lest the nursing staff should get them confused. I greeted Mom with hugs and smiles when I saw her, "I have a son! I have a son! You're a Grand-mom!"

We walked over to see Shawn. We stood transfixed in front of him, speechless. A vision meant only for Mom and me. We gazed tirelessly unable to move or look away for fear that he would change; we didn't want to miss a moment of this message.

"He is an absolute clone of Pop," Mom noticed. "He has his face, his expression, and even his barrel chest!"

I held Mom's hand and uttered, "Pop's here."

We both sobbed quietly, knowing with absolute certainty that Pop was making his presence known to comfort us, and to let us know that he wouldn't have missed this for anything. The look lasted but a few hours, but it would last far longer, forever etched into our minds.

As Mom and I visited that day, she began to remember how she and Pop met . I listened as she retold their history...

They met in the early 1930's. Sammy was casually friendly with Annabelle Pinski and her circle of friends, so it was through her that he met her sister, Flora, when Sammy was hanging out with his friends in Logan one weekend. He was a ruggedly handsome product of the era with just twenty years of life to his name. The swept back hair, à la Bogart, with his bright, blue eyes and five-foot-eight-inch lean almost wiry stature exuded an air of confidence (even with a lack of financial security) during the times of economic depression. He was a force with which to be reckoned and respected. There was a curious familiarity in his walk—an I-can-do-anything air that emanated from this young Turk.

This was not just a chance encounter; it was destiny. Flora was on a date with another young man from the neighborhood. In the midst of a collage of friends, she was introduced to this newly arrived personality in the clique. She was somewhat impressed but a trifle leery of this good-looking and very forward young man. They spoke for a bit in a very non-territorial fashion and went their opposite ways that summer evening. A connection had been made but it was far stronger on his part than hers.

At the shy and innocent age of seventeen, Flora was having a wonderful, carefree time with no intention of getting serious with anyone. He, on the other hand, after just one encounter with her, postulated with certainty that he had just met the girl he was going to marry. The wheels had been set in motion and there would be no turning back. To know Sammy was to be aware that when he made a statement, it would happen one way or another. He had the will of iron and the determination of a mule. Of course, Flora had a totally different course set and he was not part of her plans for the future. However, she was no match for the relentless spirit with whom she had just crossed paths.

Mom's sisters and brothers had come from Erie to live with some cousins about a year after their father died of pneumonia at the scant age of forty-seven. Their father had immigrated from Russia as a young man where he had been a musician in the Tzar's army. No one ever really knew how he escaped and made it to the States.

Eve, the oldest sister, got a job at Sears and several years later found an after school position there for Flora. Annabelle got involved with community theater and acting while going to school and years later pushed herself into local and state politics. They had all attended the middle and high schools but were not able to follow with college as monies were too precious and no one could afford the luxury.

In the meanwhile, Flora was enjoying Sam's persistent and unrelenting attention. His smile was infectious and comforting. Gradually, she lowered her resistance and actually allowed his charm to make her happy as she succumbed to his overtures. She learned that he was not the brusque, cocky, and brash guy she had misperceived him to be when they first met. He was just determined and would not settle for anything less than what he'd set his sights upon. "No" was not part of his personality and his instinct was as pure and focused as anyone she'd ever known. His heart had already fallen well into her and she was drawn to him in a way she'd never felt. She still resisted exclusivity since she was so young and perceived a whole world yet to be explored. He had no money to speak of and she wasn't ready to settle down, let alone struggle. Not that she was financially elite, but she and her three brothers and two sisters all had jobs and were at least making a living during that deplorable depression era.

As they talked and enjoyed each other's company, something grander than the both of them was beginning to evolve. She was falling hard and couldn't stop herself. He was warm, courteous, and nurturing with his wry non-stop humor. She was basking in the comfort of his affection and felt a sense of security that had been absent in her life. There was an ever-present sense of safety and a widening glimpse through the window of his "anything is possible" demeanor to a place that was telescoping them toward the union of their souls. The mutual draw pulled them together irresistibly with a permanence that would become their life in a new world. A marriage ceremony was conducted in the rabbi's study with close family only.

They hopped into their brand new station wagon, stopped at Horn & Hardart for dinner. Next, they drove to DC and then to Florida for their Honeymoon. A flyer in their windshield wiper boasted the arrival of a brand new hotel. They checked into it and stayed for the princely sum of a dollar and fifty cents per night. After about ten days, when the little monies they had were all but dissipated, they drove back to Philadelphia. A meager one dollar remained to their name.

No worries though, Sammy was a survivor and success was his brand. He and his father went knocking on doors everywhere asking the homeowners if they had any gold, jewelry, or anything else they would sell. Buying scraps for as little as possible, they would sell them for whatever profit they could make. They parlayed their beginning acquisitions into a business of buying and selling jewelry and antiques and eventually opened a shop downtown on 9th Street. They worked tirelessly in the depression era. Hours were whatever was necessary from dawn until late evening. They plodded on as if there were no tomorrow for if they gave in to fatigue, or the heat, or so many of the other obstacles with which they were confronted, there would have been no tomorrow. Desperation was a motivator like none other; survival was their essential instinct.

Flora and Sam lived with Sam's parents and brother and sister in their house on 19th Street until the lack of boundaries and privacy grew intolerable. Barging in on them at will was thought appropriate by Dave and Rose, Sam's parents. Miriam, his haughty sister would think nothing of walking into their bedroom without so much as a salutatory knock first. It became so commonplace that Sammy began to lock their door. Oh, what an outrage that created. How dare they! Feathers ruffled and emotions held hostage, the message was clear and present. They needed to move without delay. Their new life together was being eroded by parental and sibling inconsideration and the usurping of their very right to exist with free will.

They found an apartment for forty-seven dollars a month and moved into their own domain. They stayed there for a slight bit more than twelve months and then moved into an airlite on Champlost Street, which they were able to rent for not much more than the apartment. With space to expand, they would have children and start a family of their own. They liked the other side of the street far better though, so when 1819 Champlost became available for sale, they bought it without an instant of hesitation. Sixty-five hundred dollars was a lot of money but the move would prove to be a good one. No mortgage, just ownership in one fell swoop. Sammy never believed in encumbrances. If he wanted it, he simply bought it. No payments. He'd lived through enough financial hardship and would not be beholden to anyone. If they couldn't afford it, they didn't buy it. They just waited until they could afford it and then bought it. No one was ever going to leash him and hold him ransom again.

They accrued a fair amount of money over time as a result of their arduous work. Champlost Street in Oak Lane was a quiet family neighborhood where kids played step ball and wire ball and pedaled up and down the driveway riding their tricycles. Baseball cards were flipped, winners took all, and summer camp on the street was a way of life. Sycamore trees lined both sides of the street framing the sidewalk and created allergens every August as their bark peeled off and speckled their trunks like camouflage. The grocer was at the corner near the general store, the butcher, the bakery and the drug store. Everything was a block away at the farthest. Everyone was on first name basis, and times were friendly. The trolley turned at the corner with a soothing squeal as it braked for passengers entering and stepping off onto the cobblestone street.

Mom and Pop in Paris c. 1960

The sounds of the street were reassuring. It was the mid 1940's and the war was over. People rejoiced and headed for what they hoped would be more prosperous times. Penicillin had been discovered so fewer deaths from pneumonia and other diseases prevailed. Life was moving forward at a new pace, but hard work was still a prerequisite. Amenities like the air conditioner would soon be on the options list. New small electrical appliances were on the verge of creation; horizons brimmed with optimism. It was a post-war era of renewed growth and cautious excitement. The automobile was about to be redesigned and become more readily accessible. Air travel was on the edge of advancement. Worlds were about to narrow at a much brisker pace than ever before. Televisions were the hottest new luxury and even though color wouldn't be conceived for quite a few years, radio broadcasts were taking second position to the excitement of visual communication.

Alan, was born in 1940. He was a gorgeous platinum blond ringlet-haired sickly child with asthma and a sundry of allergies that made him a regular at the emergency room until he outgrew them. Bruce was born in 1943. He was also a blond-haired blue-eyed gorgeous combination of his parents. He was of larger stature than his older brother, but possessed a sweetness akin to that of a sleeping giant. The family antiques business was growing too and had moved to a building Sammy and his dad purchased in a superior location in the 1600 block of Pine Street. There was a lot of dealer trade, but clients like the Dupont family were also on the docket. Antique furniture moved in and out like wholesale goods. Great American pieces like Chippendale chairs and Philadelphia pie crust tables were more the norm than the exception. Highboys and Cadwallader pieces were available along with other great Philadelphia-crafted works. Salem-crafted furniture made an occasional appearance as did Queen Anne and great Louis XIV and XV masterworks.

I entered the scene January 30, 1949 as an unexpected but very loved addition to the family. There are six years difference in age between Bruce and me, and nine years difference between Alan and me, but none of that mattered. We were one family who always looked out for each other. Alan was the protector of his younger brother Bruce, who was fiercely protective of me. It was an unwritten law of instinct that unless you wanted to incur the wrath of retaliation from an older sibling, you left well enough alone and picked someone besides the David boys to taunt. The streets had their own laws and ways of defending themselves.

I was the blue-eyed, blond-haired kid who wandered up and down the street knocking on doors to say hello to the assimilation of neighbors. They all thought I was so damned cute, they all fed me like a puppy. I would come home at dinner time and Mom would be puzzled as to why I was never hungry. One day I threw up and told her of the various and sundry items I had sampled at this one's and that one's house. Suddenly it was abundantly clear. "New Shoes" as one neighbor called me because of my new sneakers, was the subject of feeding time whenever I happened by. Of course, being the shy polite young man, I could never decline and offend anyone's dignity.

⮞⮜

Chapter Sixteen

Martha Walter

⮞⮜

There was a woman named Martha Walter whose works and markets we followed closely after Pop died. Upon Martha's passing in 1976, I was reminded of how Pop had first discovered her collection.

In the cooler days of the waning summer of 1968 Mom and Pop were in a museum in North Carolina strolling through the collections with the director when Pop spied a brightly-colored beach scene hanging on a nearby wall in the corner.

"Whose work is that?" Pop queried the director with puzzlement.

"That's by Martha Walter. Don't you know her? She lives in Glenside. She's your neighbor."

Having never heard of her was astonishing enough, but Pop was stunned by this revelation of extraordinary talent. Her work looked like Mary Cassatt, Eugene Boudin, and Cecilia Beaux in one gesture of elegance and deftly-placed brush strokes. He was overwhelmed and knew he had to find her and get an exclusive representation.

As soon as he got back to Philadelphia, Pop began calling her number, which was easily found but impossible to get through to as she had a party line phone and was always talking on it. In true Sam David tradition, he drove to her house on a Sunday afternoon. Unannounced, he walked up to her door with cautious excitement and pushed the buzzer on the old, rotting, paint-worn frame. The discolored very off-white curtain on the window parted slightly as two dark suspicious eyes peered out to see who dared encroach upon her. Seeing that it wasn't someone who appeared dangerous, the short-statured old woman opened the door and with eyes of steel spoke, "Yeah, what do you want?"

Pop smiled at her and said, "I'm Sam David from the David David Gallery. I saw one of your paintings in a museum in North Carolina and fell in love. I had to meet you and see what other paintings you have. Your work is among the very best we've ever seen."

The rigid front she first adorned melted like day-old snow under the warming sun. She opened her door and waved him in as she beamed with new pride. Her dark dress dragged across the floor leaving a wake of parted dust as she led the way through the living room and motioned for him to sit down. The house smelled musty, the air ringing with a hundred-year-old history. The original 1920's furniture sat on old random-width flooring and had held but a few visitors through the years. There were paintings stacked everywhere, leaving barely a path to meander from room to room. The house was an airlite, which by design had three rooms on the first floor. The living room led into the dining room that led to the kitchen. An airlite was supposed to be airy and light. The rooms in this house were almost dark with the old lace curtains closed.

"So, what is it that you want from me?" Martha shot back. "Must be pretty damned important if you just show up at my door and don't even call first."

"I tried to call you for two days but could not get through," he defended. Martha smirked wryly. "I was intrigued with your paintings and wanted to see what others you might have available. I see you've got quite a few around here."

Truth was they lined every room in the house: the living room, dining room, bedrooms, basement, even the bathrooms, and the hallways. There was scarcely a space that wasn't covered with unframed canvases stacked ten, fifteen, and even twenty deep. Rusted nails protruded from the stretchers to which the paintings were poorly mounted. There were varying subjects: American and European beach scenes, stunning portraits of women, children, babies, garden scenes, still-life, and even a stunning series of Ellis Island paintings she had done in 1921-1922 from life. They were emotional masterworks! She captured every mood of the immigrants in the detention rooms where they prayed for admittance into the United States and waited for their names to be called. They swarmed Martha when she set up camp with her easel, paints, brushes, and palette. Mystically, they felt that if they were painted, then they would be admitted. If nothing else, they were immortalized. Most were allowed through, except those two percent determined "unqualified." Martha had a permit which authorized her to come and paint for only one Sunday afternoon but she was determined to finish the series she envisioned and forged her permit for six months of Sundays. She created a multinational collection of forty-two panels depicting the melting pot of people who would in years hence become the movers and shakers who would reshape our nation. Jewish, Italian, Spanish, German, Slavic, Chinese, and combinations thereof were stilled by the interpretation of this artist who was so inexhaustibly drawn to crowds. These folks came with nothing, many not even able to speak the language. The clothes on their back was all they owned. They had no job, no money—destitute by any measure—but they had an undefeatable will to survive and to succeed. Using the finely honed skills they brought with them from the old country, these tailors, blacksmiths, cobblers, bakers, hat makers, and farmers managed with whatever work they found and struggled against all odds to make it.

Twenty-four of the paintings depicted scenes of the various detention rooms filled with different nationalities. The other eighteen paintings were of the babies in the health station at Ellis Island where the newborns were inoculated, cared for, and readied for citizenship in the new world. Martha named the group of forty-two works "The Series" although she continued to execute another dozen or so views of the interiors of the crowded detention rooms. These instantly became a document in living history, providing us a glimpse into the microcosm of an era that was forever over in 1923.

After endless hours of frustration and several more visits, Martha finally succumbed to Pop's sincerity and pleading to give her a major exhibition with the promise of renewed fame and fortune. He assured her of becoming a household name in the art world and told her that her work was universally appealing. He promised to pay for all of the expenses of conservation, framing, and publicity in exchange for exclusive representation. She and Pop signed an informal contract scribbled on a yellow legal pad.

Pop envisioned a major success and started with about seventy-five paintings for the first exhibition. There were magnificent wispy, colorful, windblown beach scenes with mothers and children under parasols painted in New England along the sun-dappled coast of Gloucester interspersed with beautiful paintings of mothers, nursemaids, and children. There were jewel-like works of the Luxembourg Gardens in Paris from the teens.

Martha studied under William Merritt Chase at his summer studio at Shinnecock, Long Island and at the Pennsylvania Academy in 1895. She won the first Cresson prize ever given to a woman there and was able to travel to Europe to attend the Grande Chaumiere in Paris where she utilized the critical counsel of Rene Menard and Lucien Simon. However, their rigid academic approach interfered so she enrolled at the Academie Julien. A brief time later she grew weary of the restrictions of tradition and left to establish an independent studio in Paris with several other American women artists. From 1900 to 1914, she worked with many of the French icons like Renoir, so her style was decidedly French in that era. Her paintings typically expressed sophisticated color and form—replete with soft atmosphere and diffusion, evoking the delicious flavor so derivative of the romance of early Paris. They exuded contentment and ease as they portrayed the delicate interpretation of this artist's vision of beauty as she experienced it.

Exhibitions of her works go back as far as 1922 at the Gallery Georges Petit and 1924 at the Salon D'Automne, both in Paris. Her paintings are in the permanent collection of the Louvre, the Musee Du Luxembourg, the Pennsylvania Academy of the Fine Arts, the Art Institute of Chicago, Detroit Institute of Arts, Milwaukee Art Center, Toledo Museum of Art, Woodmere Art Museum in Philadelphia, and the Terra Museum in Chicago and in Giverny. She had studios in Paris, New York, Philadelphia, and Gloucester.

When Pop was having the paintings cleaned at our conservator in New York, Victor Hammer of Hammer Galleries came in to pick up some paintings for his gallery. He stopped in his tracks when he saw the Martha Walter panels and grabbed Pop's arm.

"Sammy, you've got to give me a show. These are incredible. Let's do a partnership exhibition; we'll launch it in New York and then send it to Philadelphia."

Walter Yellow Chairs

Pop was quite cognizant of the value her work would bring if it took off in New York. With Victor's enthusiasm it couldn't miss.

"Let's talk," he answered.

Victor and Pop structured a deal on the spot and began to chart the course of what would grow into generations of stunning successes for Martha and her work. The New York exhibition was a smashing success—a virtual sellout with prices ranging from $2,500 to $25,000. Our show in Philadelphia was even grander as she was a hometown phenomenon with a history from the Pennsylvania Academy, the Philadelphia Museum, the Woodmere Museum, and others. The prices of our paintings were in a similar range and shared a glorious success in sales. Opening night starred Martha herself. The press was out in numbers and a couple hundred patrons clamored to meet this 93-year-old virtuoso and vie for her paintings. It was a cocktail reception with champagne flowing freely and tray after tray of hors d'oeuvres served by butlers. Martha was beaming at the fuss and frenzied excitement. People were unwittingly swathing her ego as they fawned over her. This demurely dressed dynamo was as sharp as a tack and didn't miss a trick. She knew she was good and was quite pleased to see that her talents were being recognized, honored, and fought over with more than one instance of fierce rivalry over the same painting, leaving one client ecstatic and another forlorn.

Martha Walter English Girl

There would be many more exhibitions in subsequent years, so ultimately everyone who wanted to own a Martha Walter painting would have their wish granted and their desires fulfilled. On occasion, Pop would beg Martha to sign a painting that she'd left unsigned, explaining that this was something clients wanted.

"I will not," she huffed arrogantly. "They'll know it's my work."

Pop waded gently through her fortressed ego until she somewhat reluctantly acceded to his request to authorize her unsigned paintings when she finally realized it would widely extend her market awareness.

There was a horde of paintings sufficient to last through many years of exhibitions. The paintings were eye candy and soul soothing with their pastel colors, breezy iconography, and delicious style. Over and over again her oil paintings, watercolors, and even a few monotypes made it to market with ease. There seemed to be no end in sight to the success of her works as the prices grew steadily and demand stayed constant. But as with all good things, her market was growing a bit saturated and popular tastes were wavering a bit. Shortly after Pop died, we let Hammer Galleries deal with this expecting artist whose ego had grown insatiable. We sat back and watched as a few more exhibitions were created in New York and then slowly the ugly head of retrograde seemed to be reaching out to Martha as if to say, "Enough!"

When Martha died in 1976 at nearly 101 years, she had accomplished incredible success and lived to see it as she reaped the reward of her wonderful artistic talents. Not having heard anything about Martha Walter in months, I began to wonder what was going on with her work. I called her grand nieces to see if we could buy whatever unmarketed paintings were left of her work.

Marge and her sister Janet were interested in selling. They were in the fourth year of a five-year contract with Hammer and were eager to relinquish the deal due to the sustained high values, insurance costs, and fears of theft. Alan and I set up a time to peruse the painting collections in their storage. With contained excitement and subdued enthusiasm, we looked through stacks of unseen paintings and boxes of virgin inventory that had never been exposed to prying eyes outside of their immediate family. We told the sister we were interested in buying the entire collection, but they needed to allow Victor Hammer to make his offer first since they had been dealing with him recently. They would call us after they received Victor's offer and we tendered our number to them.

Ten days later, we got the call from Marge.

"What do you want to pay for Martha's collection?"

I gave her an amount that would secure the deal for us. Alan and I had planned this with surgical precision. There was dead silence on the other end of the line after I made the offer. Maybe we miscalculated. Maybe we are so far under the mark we lost the deal. Maybe we.....

"It's yours. Congratulations!" Came the excited response from Marge.

It turned out that we had offered three times the amount Victor offered. Sometimes you have step up and pay for what you want in life. What goes around, comes around.

We had our attorneys draw up the necessary contracts. Then, we rented a truck and went from one house to the other loading up the loose paintings and countless boxes of other paintings. There was no more room in the truck when we were finished. At midnight we took the truck back to the gallery and unloaded it. The inventory filled the gallery and there was barely enough space to see out the front showroom window. Stacks of canvases of all sizes covered every square inch of space.

The paintings all had to be cleaned, relined, and re-varnished, but otherwise they were in excellent condition. Frames had to be made for every painting. The French Impressionist gold-leafed frames with corners and sweeps took about six to eight weeks to fashion and conservation took at least the same, if not more time.

Over the next months, we organized a major retrospective exhibition using many of the best quality works of all subjects. This was going to be the first major show for Martha in quite a while and it had to be a stunner. No expense spared as we prepared for a major theatrical production which would draw the crowds with eager checkbooks. The promotional materials couldn't be designed or ordered until the paintings had been returned from our conservator in New York. They needed to be photographed for placement in a mock layout for design creation while the copy was inserted. Background colors had to be correct so they would enhance but not detract from the images of the paintings.

After all of the preliminary work was complete, the advertising needed to be placed nationally and locally. The major art journals into which we would place ads also had a six week lead time. We would forward the color transparencies to them and they would make the separations and design the ads for us and send a proof for us to authorize. Hopefully it would have the correct colors appearing when the magazines hit our target markets. Too many times the images in the magazine pages were far enough off from the true colors that it negatively affected the response. We couldn't afford for that to happen after investing this kind of expense. Between the initial purchase cost of the paintings in Martha's estate, which was steep enough in itself, coupled with the overall production expenses to make this exhibition, we were well into serious levels of six figures. We needed to recover our capital at the opening gate. The invitations went out several weeks prior and the RSVPs came in quickly with almost no regrets. We were expecting about two hundred or so excited guests.

It was a beautiful, clear autumn day and the temperatures were just right at sixty degrees and no humidity. The exhibition, "Martha Walter, A Retrospective" was set to open sharply at five o'clock. We had staff members on both the first and second floors with trays of hors d'oeuvres. There were bartenders at stations on both floors. Our walls were filled with magnificent, colorfully-balanced Impressionist paintings priced from $7,500 to $75,000. The lines began to form at our front doors as patrons vied for position to have first choice of the paintings. An armed guard stood by as we opened the doors to let the swarming crowd inside to preview the unseen works of Martha Walter.

Red dots were added to the labels as the paintings were sold. And sell they did. Over the course of the three-hour reception, all but a handful of works remained unsold. At the end of the evening we collected all the checks and breathed an exhilarating sigh of relief. Our vision of success unfolded as we had anticipated. We recovered a serious chunk of capital, and this was the birth of a series of exhibitions which would continue to generate revenue for the foreseeable future.

The exhibition was to be open to the public the next day and continue for the next few weeks, but there was nothing left of the premier line of inventory! We filled the empty walls with the second wave of inventory we had waiting in the wings.

One night when Arlyn and I were watching late night television, there was a plea for help in finding missing children as their pictures were displayed on the sides of milk cartons. We knew we had to produce an exhibition of the "Children of Martha Walter" as a benefit for the National Center for Missing and Exploited Children in Washington, DC. We had scads of fabulous paintings of children and babies by Martha just waiting to go to market. With large organizations, you never know if they will respond favorably but we had to offer our idea to them regardless. It was a completely different approach than advertizing on milk cartons. This culture and event could generate much more significant funding for the center. They loved our idea and were grateful for our generosity. They agreed to provide the catering and the venue, which turned out to be the Arts Club. We planned and publicized a reception in Washington with the press attending. We created and funded the printing of the catalogue, and delivered the inventory. Linda Carter (Superwoman) was our spokesperson at the opening and a good many paintings of happy children sold. The exhibition was a stunning success and we were able to donate ten percent of the proceeds which was a significant sum of money.

We tied several of the next exhibitions to charities like the Red Cross and the Burn Foundation of the Delaware Valley at the gallery in Philadelphia where we hosted the cocktail receptions. At each fanfare, the sales were equally impressive. Many exhibitions, both on site and at other galleries under our quiet direction, followed for years to come.

At the close of the 1990's, we re-evaluated the balance of the existing inventory and made a decision to begin gradually pulling back and place the entire remains into other hands. It was a significant move for us as there was still plenty of market money left in the deal, but it was more important to us to protect our long-term client relationships and walk away from the remaining paintings that were not representative of Martha's best quality. We do, however, still deal in Martha's works as we cherry pick the markets for her best quality and when they come back to us for resale from our generational client list.

Chapter Seventeen

A Late Message

For many years throughout the 1950's and 1960's, Pop had done business with Frank Reedy of McClees Gallery in Ardmore, a quaint little bedroom community suburb of Philadelphia along the Main Line. Named for the train that serviced the area, the Main Line is a relatively affluent and desirable area that provides easy access to the city and yet it is totally suburban, serene, quite and elegant. Sandwiched neatly between Haverford and Wynnewood, McClees dealt in American and European eighteenth to twentieth century paintings for the most part. They also had a working conservation facility in the lower level of the shop where they did light cleaning, relining, and more extensive restoration as necessary.

Frank would refer clients to Pop and he would take care of him with generous referral fees when he closed a deal with the client. Frank's son Michael was in the shop learning his dad's business and taking some of the work upon himself. It was another father and son transference in the making. They were a landmark in the area and enjoyed a wonderful reputation.

A year or two after Pop's passing, Michael, then touching thirty, came into our gallery with a somewhat uncomfortable look about him. It was otherwise just another uneventful day but there was a disquieting sense in the air. Michael wore his usual uniform: jeans, a hound's tooth blazer, and a pair of well-worn and somewhat misshapen brown loafers. His bright blue eyes were blazing, and his black hair—partially swept back was interspersed with grey that feathered in nicely. He gave me a warm hug hello and clutched me as a long lost friend.

"Could I talk with you for a few minutes?" He was a bit squirmy, and I sensed his uneasiness.

"It would be a pleasure."

He looked around the room. "Are we were alone in the gallery?"

"Yes...... Are you okay?"

He nodded his head gently and shrugged. "I have to tell you something that has been on my mind for a couple of years now."

My palms grew clammy. What could he possibly need to tell me?

"I never wanted to upset you, so..." Michael sat down. "I've held back. I but can't any longer."

I was perplexed and a bit on edge not knowing what I was going to hear. I did not suspect it was going to be good news for his demeanor indicated otherwise. He rocked from side to side clasping his hands in preparation for what he was about to disclose. His brow beaded with tiny droplets of moisture. He took a deep breath, looked me squarely in the eyes and offered, "I was in London late summer of 1973 and had a dream one night that was so vivid and real, I was convinced it was much more than a dream. I was in my room when out of a long dark corridor, I saw your father approaching me."

I was stilled by his words as he continued.

"He was coming toward me with the most brilliant, liquid blue eyes I'd ever seen. They were so blue that they made Paul Newman's eyes look brown. He held out his hands to show me a large, brilliant, sparkling, and blindingly bright diamond. It had what looked to be a million facets and it was dazzling with a gleaming heavenly light like I'd never seen before—just like his dancing blue eyes—riveting, but I couldn't look away. His scintillating crystal blue eyes of fire froze me. It was breathtaking, like the diamond he so proudly held out to show me. He smiled an endless smile that beamed with the same light that overcame everything in its path. There was nothing but light, pure love, and infinite happiness. And then, just as mysteriously as he appeared, he suddenly drew backward away from me, locking eyes with me like the penetrating glowing brilliance of a dying supernova. Then, he was gone."

"And then.....?" I hungered for more.

"I awoke infused with the fullness of his brilliance imprinted upon me. I felt so wonderfully calm and full of peace. I couldn't tell if I just had a dream or if it was some kind of vision. You know I studied Edgar Cayce and his writings for years, and yet I was stunned and left wondering. I am no stranger to metaphysical phenomenon but I had never experienced anything with this much power."

"Wow!"

"There's more," he paused. "It gets even more bizarre. I went back to life as usual for the next couple of weeks but I couldn't stop thinking of the vision that so embraced me. I was due for a visit back to the States so I made the airline reservations, packed up my stuff and after an uneventful flight, made it home for the Labor Day holiday at the end of August. I was really looking forward to seeing my folks. I hadn't been stateside for months and really missed them. I hopped a cab at the airport and thirty minutes later, Mom and Dad greeted me at the door with warm hugs. I took my bags upstairs, washed up, and came down for a wonderful home-cooked dinner my Mom had eagerly prepared in anticipation of my arrival home. The aroma of the food was intoxicating and welcoming for sure. As we sat and ate and sipped our scotch, my father looked at me with an unsettling reluctance in his glance, as if there was something he needed to tell me. I sensed his discomfort and tilted my head with an inquiring motion, 'Dad, what is it?'

'I hate to be the bearer of bad news,' Dad said, 'but Sam David passed away.' He paused delicately. 'I wanted you to hear it from me, and not from someone on the street.'

"I was stunned. He was so young and vibrant. How could this be? I really felt close to your dad, remembering all the times he'd come into our little gallery bringing a welcome breeze with him. His energy was contagious, his smile infectious, his way so comforting and reassuring. He just made me feel good." Michael raised his head, "I was overcome with sadness. I'd lost a good friend. Dad told me how it happened and said Sam had died on August first, about two weeks prior. A numbing chill enshrouded me as the image of his brilliant hypnotic azure eyes and the blinding light from the super-faceted diamond began to make perfect sense. He was showing me that even in death, life goes on and that he was at peace, perfectly content, and vivid in the light of the universe; that the possibilities in life were without end, that love abounded and nothing is final; that we continue in the all encompassing light, a never-ending source of comfort. I was to live my life and when the time was right, convey this message to you so you'd know he is all right.

"I don't know why your dad came to me instead of you." Michael was uneasy and I could tell he felt a bit of guilt that he had been visited by my father. "I feel like the time was right and I was supposed to tell you now."

"Thank you for coming to me and relating this encounter. It means more than you know. My tears are a consolation, and not because of sadness."

Michael smiled with relief. "I'm glad I didn't upset you." He embraced me as a kindred spirit.

The message of Pop's brilliance in eternity was meant for me. Yes, the time was exactly right.

Chapter Eighteen

Rack 'Em

After a while, perhaps nearly six years after pop's death, I decided one day to put away his watch that I had been wearing. I had from the onset felt peculiar about the possibility of having caused Mom a revival of anguish, and by this time I had begun to tire of wearing Pop's watch. I wanted my own. His had taken on the appearance of a toy, so I decided that it was time for a serious change. I went out that day and chased down the Rolex I really wanted which was the 18-carat gold one with the president's bracelet. I was going to be thirty years old that winter and felt I had earned it, so I took a good chunk of our savings and invested in it. I had been in love with that watch for years but had neither the capital nor the maturity to handle it. As it turned out, the gift actually came from Arlyn because it was purchased with money we had saved together to spend on something in the future.

I was totally thrilled with my new acquisition. I had put the past into proper perspective and set my sights on the future. The clock was running and I didn't wish to be trampled in its wake. I no longer needed to hold on to the past; I needed to break the old chains and run like the hammers of hell. I had to find out exactly how far I could push my own success without standing in my father's shadow.

Of course, this event brought back memories of the times I had spent with Pop. He was so spontaneous. He'd be sitting stretched on the sofa in the living room with his shoes and socks off, and his face hidden by the newspaper he'd settled in to read after dinner. I never knew when Pop might be in the mood to shoot pool and blurt out a request for a partner.

"Let's go flying," he would shout with enthusiasm, or "Let's make milkshakes," or "Let's play chess," or the ultimate challenge, "Let's shoot pool!" My blood would race. I loved the game and always hungered to play.

The toughest obstacle was Mom's dogmatic refrain, "It's a school night, Sam!"

"Aw come on," he charmed. "I won't keep him out too long. Hey, why don't you come with us?" He suggested tauntingly.

"No, that's okay; just don't be late." She had no desire to hang around a billiard parlor with a bunch of indelicate, foul-mouthed, frustrated teenaged toughs.

We grabbed our coats and scrambled out the door into the winter darkness, aiming the car toward 19th and Cheltenham to the hallowed halls of the old Cue and Cushion. I prayed it wouldn't be too crowded. Sometimes there was an hour or better wait for a table. The low life would linger outside in the parking lot, sitting on the hoods of neighboring cars. Not ours though; if they attempted it, a mild but firm directive from Pop to remove themselves would quickly scatter them. He had a way of making his point very clear so people respected and obeyed, even if they were of significantly larger stature.

That night the place wasn't crowded; in fact, we had a choice of tables. The only real difference besides the location was the degree of wear in the felt, and they were all pretty well worn, but still decent. Most were Formica railed with green felt; some with gold. We made our choice and proceeded to hunt for cue sticks with least amount of warp. They all seemed to have as many curves as a mountain road, but after searching and sighting along the sticks like rifle barrels while rotating them, we found a couple...with tips even!

Pop racked the first one and let me break, but with the understanding that it'd likely be the last break I'd get all night. I nodded patronizingly with defiance. He was damned good, and it was always a humiliating struggle for me to exceed his highly developed skill. He had been playing since he was a kid, and winning too! I couldn't have asked for a better teacher. He was a great example to follow; he was kind, inspiring, and filled with enthusiasm for the sport and for me. He'd point out the proven methods for success: the ease of the long, slow stroke with geometric precision; the English left and right, follow and draw, combination shots, usage of the bridge; how to rack the balls tightly, and how to break them; playing them safe or wide open. I'd get frustrated when my shots were off, but what I was too young to know was that my game was off because I was off. The game can only be a reflection of one's emotional state, and though skill plays the predominant part of mastering the game, emotional togetherness holds a critical piece of the pie.

I admired Pop for not allowing me to win. By doing so, he forced me to play more seriously. Many times, he nudged me into a corner where I was choking on my own frustration. There was only one avenue—the intelligent one, not the impulsive one that came from instinct, but rather of wisdom. I learned a bit more slowly than I want to admit, but looking back, I wasn't any less stubborn or persistent than any other child that age. Now, I see the very same traits in my kids, and it's totally frustrating when I try and spare them the shortsightedness that I've worked so arduously for years to exorcise. But, if they aren't allowed to fumble through it and discover for themselves that it doesn't work, they'll never be able to see the obstacles, let alone overcome them.

For me, frustrations and barriers have always presented a thrill. The sweetness of one's successes are commensurate with the degree of difficulty in getting there. If something is too easy, it seems like any idiot could achieve it; there's no special quality about it, but when a major hurdle is overcome, there comes with it a genuine sense of achievement.

Shooting pool was only one of many ways I was taught that lesson, and now I pass on the knowledge to my two junior sharks, who cannot understand why the obvious sure shot is not always the best choice. I frequently overlook it for the more intriguing triple combination which they nod in agreement is totally impossible.

"Dad, you're crazy," they chide, "The five is dead in the side pocket."

They jump up and down like jellybeans with excitement and sarcasm, assured in their own minds that it's already their turn. I've calculated the shot; allowed for error; walked around the table twice, lined it up as I bent down to sight it, and gently stroked my cue to hit the combination with slight English right. I could almost have shut my eyes to hear the "kerthunk" of my victory. All mouths dropped in amazement. There was a total absence of words—a quiet of such magnitude that it was as shattering as a bolt of lightening followed by a clap of thunder. I looked up at them with a wry half-smile that reeked of self-pride. It's happened many times, and each time I could feel my father smiling from within. I swear I felt him. It was a hell of a lot more than a mannerism, or a wish, or reminiscence. It was real, frighteningly so, but reassuring, too. For an instant, I sense his presence as chills befall my body and I have to restrain the tears. *Son of a bitch. Is this real? Is he here with me? Am I dreaming? Am I certifiable?* He seems so alive; so much a part of me!

It's long been my belief that when someone dies, they're dead only in the sense that their body is lifeless, but its soul, energy, or spirit has transcended across another dimension, invisible but existent, nonetheless. The wind is an invisible force and we all know it's passing through when we feel its biting chill on a cold winter's day. We've seen the awesome force of such an invisible foe as an earthquake. Is not the phenomenon of a sound wave inexplicable to those incapable of auditory perception? When you turn on the radio, you hear the sound waves generated from the other end, but you can't see them. You can even feel them if they're loud enough, or if they carry enough bass. And there's the dog who possesses an uncanny range of hearing at considerably higher levels than ourselves. They hear things we wouldn't even if broadcast right into our faces!

How can you explain in realistic terms special effects like pre-cognitive thought, thought transference, and extrasensory perception? What we can't deal with or justify, we deny, excuse, or ignore. So, when I experience something as overwhelming as the strength of my father's spiritual presence, it's very real to me. A bit incomprehensible at times, but always welcome. I'll probably never stop missing him.

≈ ≈

Chapter Nineteen

The Visit

≈ ≈

The years had passed one by one since Pop had died. I had made fifty or more trips to New York and back, each time skirting the general direction of the cemetery which was too conveniently nearby. Every time I took that access road to the Pennsylvania Turnpike, I glanced apprehensively at the underground storage community known as Roosevelt Memorial Park to my left. I was enveloped by a peculiar mixture of fear, eagerness, and guilt when approaching the area. Sometimes I looked the other way to avoid the uncertainty altogether. I was torn between the mad desire to return to Pop's gravesite and satisfy a long-growing guilt for my absence and abandonment, and the fright of what I would or wouldn't find there. I wondered whether he would know I was there, or that I'd not been back to visit since the day of his funeral. The most gruesome of thoughts began to filter into my head. I envisioned the interior of his casket and puzzled as to whether or not there was even a shred of skin or bone left. Was there any hair or clothing which hadn't yet been vaporized by the villains of time? For how long would there remain a resemblance of his being? Could anything really penetrate the man-made tomb which lay six feet below? All questions which would have to rely on my imagination for their solution.

One morning, I had to make a delivery of a painting to a client in Summit, New Jersey, which would take me right past the cemetery. There was no time to stop even if I had wanted to, because I had to get to this client before he left for a weekend trip to the country. I started out early enough to land me in Summit in an hour and a half. My plan was to drop the painting to the client, pick up a check, and get back to Philadelphia as quickly as possible.

I hadn't directly calculated a stop at the cemetery, but I had the feeling that my unconscious had already made the arrangements. I was running on overdrive. I had finished my appointed rounds for the morning and the day was still young; barely ten hours old. I didn't care to saunter through this affluent and neatly manicured area of the world. Something more significant was reaching out to me. There was yet another summit to conquer: the final resting place of my father.

The morning was quite cool, offering a sparkling blue sky with the June breeze carrying the hint of summer just beyond the last breaths of spring. Most of the flowering trees and shrubs had shed their colorful coats of glorious petals and had conformed to the uniform gradations of greenery they proudly displayed. I marveled at the perpetual cycle of life which they demonstrated. For them, every year would begin life all over again. As we changed seasons, so do they. But, they seemed planted so firmly, and with such permanence, unlike the participants of their counterparts in the human league. Some trees were capable of sustaining life for hundreds and hundreds of years. But alas, at some point they too would be felled by one of nature's obstacles. Perhaps it would be man himself who would cut these towering monuments down to clear a path for his own shelter or transport, or simply an inadvertent passing storm whose wind or electricity would derail their immortality with a swift and ruthless strike. The more I pondered the existence of the foliated universe around me at the cemetery, the more aware I became of the vulnerability of our own life's lease. The one thing which we unwittingly shared with all specimens on the planet was the limit on our time here on Earth.

The cemetery had many entrances, none of which I could chose with any inkling of pleasure. It had been years since I had seen this God-forsaken land, and I didn't really know where I was headed. I knew the gravesites were in a specific section so I drove through the open gates and let my memory steer me through the labyrinth of marble architecture. Gradually, it began to look uncomfortably familiar. I took turn after turn as the monuments started to blur into a completely homogenous shape and color. Obelisks and gravestones, markers and buildings all took on the same form. They were frozen pieces of time that had been erected as tribute to loved ones, but which now stood alone and grew cold with time as the years marched forward. They decorated the landscape with the same deadness as those for whom they were dedicated. They appeared as gray limbless marble trees aiming at the sky. Some had tilted to one direction or another, and others had toppled from old age or neglect. Their morbidity was merely a parallel to life—a silent but visually powerful reminder of the end that can never be predicted with any more than random accuracy.

The knot in my stomach was ever tightening and a cold sweat was pouring over my entire body. My hands were icy and my skin was bloodless and pale. My breath became short and I trembled with a fear impossible to control. I was within yards of the most punishing reality I ever had to face, but it wasn't within me to turn and run. I found a strength that gave me the will to push onward and get out of the car to walk the longest ten yards of my life. I wobbled in a semi-straight line to the grassy edge in front of me. I didn't know what I expected to find, but there amidst the open field were the two markers of Pop and Bruce with space between them for future accommodation. There were no tombstones or monuments. We are simple folk with no message to leave behind, except to those who are in our hearts, and they need no stone inscriptions. Everything is said while it is meaningful, not after the fact. It was with that in mind that the only identification to be left behind for any observers was a simple flat marker which bore the name and birth and death dates of the person whose remains were at rest below. There were no saccharin messages; we all carried the memories within our hearts and souls.

The feeling was far different than I had imagined. I sat down on the grass-covered foreground and felt a nourishing sense of peacefulness as I listened to the symphony of insects chanting their warm sounds in this otherwise lifeless playground. I sat next to my father's plot and began to cry softly. At first I felt the hollowing pain of his loss. All the visions of the funeral returned so vividly, it seemed like it was only yesterday. I could see the swelling crowd of mourners who approached to pay homage to a great man who was their uncle, cousin, friend, or acquaintance. I could hear the Aztec as she flew overhead and seemed to bow with reverence as if to say farewell to her master, disappearing as spontaneously as it arrived. I could hear the bereavement, even the smells of that summer day in August as I indulged myself in deep sadness. I sat motionless in a twilight zone of pity and remorse until I realized that Pop wouldn't have wanted that for me. His wish was for my happiness and for life to go on regardless of its drawbacks. I also came to the realization that his grave was only a marker. The spirit of my father was no longer there, only his body which lay buried beneath it. I was learning that my fears had been just fears, nothing more; that my father's shell was all that existed. His energy was in another space in time, in another dimension— seemingly intangible, yet only a thought away.

The experience was totally draining, but I felt the relief of having accomplished a most difficult task. I felt victorious because I had finally put something to rest. It was behind me now and I no longer carried with me the compulsion to confront a nightmare of my own creation. I had taken the challenge as Pop had taught me to do through our years together, and I had grown up all over again. In the distance, I could hear the faint resounding of life; the trucks and airplanes on their way to their destinations, the birds and insects performing their daily vigils. I began to regain my strength. I became acutely aware that there was no longer any need to return here again. My father was immortalized in my mind, and I would carry his vision forever. Death, nor anything else, could ever steal that away from me. Though I felt no necessity for another visit, I was entitled if I chose to return, but if I did, it would be without the persistent childlike fear that had prevented me from taking a giant step forward toward adulthood.

I took the privilege of one last stare as I turned to walk to the car. I felt more intact, though slightly weary, than ever before. I left the emptiness of the so called "final ground," a term to which I could no longer lend credibility, and proceeded to satisfy the symbolic void which I had induced by not ingesting any food since the night before. I had returned with a very welcome sense of inner peace.

Chapter Twenty

Our Second Son

Gatsby, our Golden Retriever must have known something was up. He had followed Arlyn around for hours and would not leave her side. Arlyn was full with child and due any day. With Shawn over four years old, we were excited to grow our family and have our next child come into our lives. Our pregnancy was smooth and uneventful save for some early morning nausea in the first few months. Arlyn radiated with beauty; motherhood was her perfect partner.

"Honey, can we just go to sleep?" I pleaded one evening in early November. "I'm exhausted."

"Sure, sweetie. Just let me check on Shawn." Arlyn soothed. "I'll be right in."

After a few moments, Arlyn returned, pulled back the sheets, and plunked into bed looking fatigued. She turned on the television and stretched out with her legs bent and her back against the pillows.

"Uh, oh" she uttered.

"What?"

"I think my water just broke!"

"You're kidding right? God, not tonight, I'm so tired, I can't see straight."

"No, I'm not kidding. The bed's soaked."

"I'm not ready."

"Yeah, well, you'd better get ready quick. I'm having a contraction!"

I jumped up, put my jeans back on, and called Mom.

"Arlyn's water just broke. Grab a cab, and hurry please!"

"I'll be there in twenty minutes," Mom assured.

"Thanks."

"I'm calling Doctor Kalodner," I yelled to Arlyn. So much for being tired or sleepy. My adrenaline had taken over.

"Okay, I'm getting my bag together. Is your Mom coming?"

"She's on her way. Don't wor.....What d'ya mean Dr. Kalodner isn't there?" I yelled into the phone at his answering service.

"Don't worry, he'll be at the hospital before you get there. He's on his way," she stated.

"Oh, okay. Thank you."

Moments later, Mom showed up to stay with Shawn. After we left for the hospital, Gatsby went into Shawn's room and didn't budge all night.

Arlyn's labor was relatively easy and the baby arrived without delay, a scant three hours after Arlyn's water bag popped. At 2:38 on November 4, 1980, just four days shy of Pop's birthday, we were blessed with our second magnificent son, Brett. He was beautiful. Blond hair, blue eyes, and weighing seven pounds four ounces. Ten toes and ten fingers, all parts intact. A sigh of relief! As I held him just out of delivery, he peed all over me just like Shawn did four years prior! Holding my sons right after they were born had to be the most thrilling moment of my life. It is inexplicable; the best high life can offer. I was elated.

A few days later when we brought Brett home from the hospital, Shawn's only complaint was, "I wanted to help make him. Why didn't you wait for me?" It would be years before he would understand.

By this time, Shawn was displaying evidence of Pop's traits and isms that he had apparently inherited. I remember when we were driving somewhere that he reached forward from his car seat to turn the radio on. He held his hand with thumb and forefinger straddling the button while the other three fingers curved and elevated away in a helix-like fashion. I'd seen my father do that in the identical fanlike pattern, when he tuned the avionics in the Aztec.

I was stunned as I said to Arlyn, "Look at that. Do you know who used to..."

"Your father," she finished before I could get the words out.

It was a pattern that Shawn repeated time and time again. He also possessed a stubbornness that he must have acquired from Pop. I wasn't sure it was such a good thing at the time, but it proved less frustrating years later when channeled properly. One day Shawn stood facing me, leaned in close with his face only inches away from mine and crossed his eyes making a silly face. Pop's trademark was written all over that gesture. He used to do that to me all the time to get me to smile. It never failed; it was too goofy not to get a laugh.

Chapter Twenty-One

First Boat

It was summer 1986 and Arlyn and I were watching the late night news. I caught a clip about the new marina opening in Philadelphia. I turned to Arlyn.

"When did this happen?"

"No idea." She shrugged.

"I'm going down there tomorrow morning to rent a slip."

"What for? We don't have a boat!"

"Not yet," I winked.

After tending to an empty slip until mid-July, we bought a wonderful twenty-seven-foot Sea Ray with twin 230-horsepower inboard/outboard engines. Since this was our first boat, we went as large as possible in our price range while staying in a size where we felt comfortable. Ease of handling was important, but having enough room not to get too cramped was also a consideration.

The day before we were to pick her up twenty miles upriver, there was the urgency to create a name, both for the transom and for registration purposes. I racked my brain until finally as I was on the drive home after work, it hit me. We'd name her "97 Yankee" in memory of Pop and the Aztec he so cherished, whose call letters were N6897Y. This would be my Aztec, and we would carry on the legend. Perhaps only a few would recognize the symbolism of the name, but the statement was out there for Pop.

It was several hours before we actually got to put the boat in water and take her down river. Everything had to be checked over, a Coast Guard inspection procured, and I had to prove my handling skills before they would release the boat into my custody. I was a little nervous at first, but after a few minutes at the controls, it was as if I'd been born into the position. We headed south for the forty-minute cruise during which time I played with the throttles, trim tabs, out drives, and whatever else could be adjusted. It was incredible to be skimming along the water at almost fifty miles per hour with the engines working at full power in roaring unison. When the throttles were opened wide on the river, the engines roared like those of an airplane. The wind in my eyes forced a slit-like visibility and my hearing was governed by the push of air as it flowed by with tremendous velocity. It was thrilling to be at the helm with my wife and sons as my father had done in his plane with his family just one generation before.

The day was hot and steamy and we were virtually alone out there. As we made our way down the river to our homeport marina, an airplane crossed the river directly above us. Normally I wouldn't have given a second look, but something in the familiar sound drew my attention. All at once, the past merged with the present in a fleeting gesture of immortality. My eyes canted upward in time to see an Aztec flying overhead. I pointed upward for Arlyn and the kids to see, and we all smiled as we bathed in its loving embrace. It dipped its wings briefly and then flew off quietly. Pop was acknowledging us and I was chilled to the bone in that ninety-degree heat. I know he was there—not a shred of doubt in my mind. And though I wasn't able to read the call letters of that airplane, I just knew they were N6897Y.

Chapter Twenty-Two

The Legend

Barely spring and in whipping winds that chilled to the bone, I moved our boat upriver from the winter marina to the summer marina, which was more spacious and provided a more interesting vista. I could hardly wait to get back on the water. It didn't matter that the mercury was in the forties and grey as twilight. After the bite of the past two months even that felt warm and inviting. It was a harbinger of the balm which was not far away.

Something felt different that day. The boat seemed to usher in a feeling of impatience. Last year's excitement was tarnished and clouded by a new yearning. I had been bitten by the proverbial bug to go bigger—the boater's nightmare of wanting something more! As I walked below deck, I felt cramped. I wanted more headroom and more room to stretch out and entertain. Thinking myself totally out of my mind, I left with a new challenge in my head. This boat, which had brought so much pleasure, had gradually lost its shine. Amazingly Arlyn was feeling the same way, so we agreed to look and see if the notion was financially within reach. Since we were coming out of a twenty-seven footer, the next logical step would be to thirty-four feet. It's incredible how expensive those extra few feet are.

The search was on in full force. I was obsessed. I called every dealer who had any degree of respect until I tumbled onto one who had what sounded to be the perfect fit. It was a dealer demo, a 1988 Wellcraft Gransport with a very few hours on it. They had used her for a few boat shows and for some reason it remained unsold. He said I could come take a look at my convenience. I was there that afternoon after work, and as soon as I saw her, it was all over. I had to have her.

I greeted Arlyn on the baseball field where Shawn's game was still in progress. I described to her what I had seen only a half hour before and I knew my excitement was causing an explosion of emotion that I could hardly control. I had the presence of mind to take a Polaroid camera with me so at least I had somewhat of a visual to validate my lunacy. We were in agreement that the boat was magnificent—white hull with black and aquamarine trim and full aquamarine canvas to complement the sleek Eurostyling with American craftsmanship—a stunning combination as was everything else about her. Twin 454 big blocks, 6.5 Onan generator, air-conditioning and heat, full galley with microwave, electric stove, and space galore. The list went on and on, and by the time we closed the negotiation a few days later we had added a few more things we considered essential. We even managed to produce a creative financial arrangement by utilizing our old boat as trade. It was 1989 and money was pretty expensive as inflation lead the way. Rates were high all over the market, but they needed to get rid of this piece of inventory and we were there with a deal in hand. It would be a stretch, but there was no turning back.

Once more we had to get creative and give the boat a name so the dealer could get it painted on the transom before we could take delivery on Saturday morning. I searched my mind endlessly and gave up for the moment. Then, it dawned on me. I again wanted to name the boat after Pop. We all agreed that the name "Legend" seemed to describe him well.

The forecast for that mid-June day was sunny, hot, and humid with temperatures tipping into the low nineties. We arrived about eleven o'clock in the morning with anticipation that made for sweaty hands. The boat was not ready so we had to impatiently wait a couple of hours. Last minute details needed completion. Marine time always means running late. If you're told an hour or so, three or four is more likely. Today can mean tomorrow, and a week or so will likely translate to mean a month! The Legend was gleaming with a luster and beauty that seemed to exceed factory specifications. She sure didn't look that large out of the water! Finally we boarded for the dedicated run through. I was shown every detail and we started up the engines—left, then right. I was in heaven! This was the sound for which I longed my entire life. Even at idle, that deep-throated burble promised not to disappoint. Those engines with cavernous side-emitting exhausts produced the most exquisite symphony of vibrations I'd ever heard. It was so strong and so sweet that my eardrums quivered with each beat of their frequency.

They wouldn't release the boat to us until I could adequately demonstrate my handling skills. We idled out to the center of the river which had a swift current with a significant opposing crosswind. I successfully accomplished every command the pilot barked to me. The boat handled beyond measure and showed integrity and ability I couldn't have imagined. It was actually easier than our old boat, which I no longer missed. The beam of twelve feet six inches found a stability that astounded me. A few more tricky maneuvers and we took the pilots back to the marina and shoved off on our own.

The feeling of exhilaration was euphoric as I pushed the throttles forward and we lifted the nose from the water. As we quickly got up on plane, the bow settled down and we all languished in the wondrous pleasure of our new friend. The noise was behind us as the landscape slipped by like a moving picture. The breezes were soothing and the heat seemed to dissipate as we moved down the river. Just as we passed the Tacony Palmyra Bridge we all looked up as one does when running under a bridge. An unexpected glitter of pure metal appeared in the sky. A couple of hundred feet above us was an Aztec airplane with no paint and no numbers emanating that unmistakable blended sound of two Lycoming engines. As with our last boat, the Aztec dipped its wings in both directions as it passed directly over us with and swiftly disappeared into the distant sky. I had a lump of emotional resistance in my throat, which stuck there until I yielded to the overpowering flood of tears that cascaded from my eyes. We all knew at a glance what this meant. It was Pop sharing our joy as he bestowed his blessing upon us. This was a significant episode that gave reassurance of Pop's spirit living on with us.

Chapter Twenty-Three

Symptomatic

Brett was growing into a warm, loving being who looked idyllically to his brother for everything. The two boys stuck together and worked beautifully in tandem as the years passed all too quickly. We were consumed with sports in every season: soccer, basketball, and baseball. Frequently, the schedules overlapped so we criss-crossed and took turns going to Shawn's and Brett's games. And then there were practices, and championship games that at times also occurred simultaneously. Good thing the fields were only five minutes apart. Those were happy days which would run into dusk and then night as the overtimes mounted and penalties abounded with frustrated players and coaches. Dinners were haphazard but no one cared. Homework still had to be done and projects finished so everything was appropriately compressed. We had so much fun and made so many friends on the sidelines of the grass chalk-marked playing fields.

Alan lost the passion for the family business and hated the twice weekly run back and forth to Philadelphia from New York where he was living. He grew more interested in the scholarly aspect of the business while I thrived on the action and the deal making. He needed a change; the business did not excite him anymore. Once he determined that I was self-sufficient, he left the business in my hands.

As I drifted off to sleep one night in late January, I felt an air of malaise. The ensuing nightmare revealed the answer. In my dream, there had been a horrible plane crash as a jumbo jet fell through the sky and totally decimated 30th Street Station, Philadelphia's main rail terminal with destinations to all points. As I watched the aftermath, I felt sick to my stomach. Remnants of the explosion were strewn about like matchsticks. Building girders were hanging in twisted memory of their former shapes. Bodies were everywhere; there was a frightening air of death and destruction in all directions. Fires were burning and smoke was lifting above what remained. The roads were crumbled, and I thought of the impossibility of getting in and out of town for months to come. The expressway was in upheaval not unlike the major interstates in San Francisco after the earthquake a couple of years back. Layers of roadway were suspended in mid-air just waiting for the slightest weight to send them careening down to the piles of smoldering rubble below. It seemed as if the slightest breeze would have affected the collapse.

My thoughts turned to Mom as a wave of panic flooded through me. Her apartment house was just outside the perimeter of the danger zone. However, I immediately knew that she was all right. I knew she was alive and unharmed, though she would be affected by this trauma.

I awoke in a sweat and couldn't stop shaking. It was so real. I had been keeping a dream journal because I knew there was valuable information present in the dream state. The challenge was to remember the experiences and to make the intuitive interpretation to decipher the coded messages. To help me remember before going back to sleep, I told Arlyn briefly about my nightmare, and promised to recount the details in the morning.

It would be a couple of weeks before the meaning of this nightmare became clear. I did know immediately though, that my birthday, January 30th, was going to unfold something awful.

Mom was closing in on her eighth decade and had been more fatigued than usual lately. She was devoid of energy and stamina coupled with a decreasing appetite. She had never been a ball of energy and had always stated, "I was born tired." True perhaps, but we all insisted that she let Dr. Marcolina, her general physician, check her out. The results of her blood work showed that Mom was somewhat anemic but there was no obvious blood loss. Dr. Marcolina was a thorough diagnostician and would not relent until she had her answers. She ordered a colonoscopy in order to cover all her bases.

Mom followed the standard protocol of the chemical salt drinks to ensure her intestines evacuated completely before the investigatory procedure could be done. I waited in the hospital waiting room for an hour or so until they brought her out of recovery. Another doctor approached me, and introduced himself as Dr. Dufresne. I knew from the look on his face that they had found something and it wasn't good.

"We found a mass on her colon and it needs to come out as soon as possible." It took a few minutes for the words to gain acceptance. Mom was becoming more awake, so Dr. Dufresne leaned over her and softly spoke to her, "We found a mass on your colon, and it needs to be removed. We feel you'll be fine. Think about it and let me know when you want to come in for the surgery."

Without even a split second's hesitation after hearing the dreadful news of a malignancy living inside her, Mom ordered, "I'm here now; let's do it today! If there is something that needs to come out, let's get rid of it. It doesn't belong there! I'm ready; let's go!"

"We can't do it today since you've just come out of anesthesia," the doctor explained, "but we can schedule it for tomorrow.

"Tomorrow then," she affirmed. Tomorrow would be January 30—my birthday—just like my dream had indicated. I had peace that Mom would be fine.

More tests were ordered in the interim. Later that afternoon in Mom's room we visited with Dr. Marcolina who told us, "I suspected a tumor had caused the anemia as it leached your mom's blood and grew into a killer. All of the team doctors feel certain that Flora is going to be okay and that we caught it early enough. However, we won't know for certain until we are in there."

Early that evening, we met with the anesthesiologist as well as the surgeon who gave us a rundown of the procedures, timelines, and so forth. We felt as comfortable as we could at that point. The next morning the operating room was reserved and set up to extract this venomous entity from Mom. The surgery began as we waited for what seemed an endless morning that turned into afternoon as the others waiting for word on their loved ones appeared and disappeared during our hours of prayers.

"Carl for Flora," the waiting room nurse summoned us. "You can pick up that phone over there and talk with the surgeon."

I raced to pick up the phone before it finished the first ring.

"Your mother is going to be fine!" The surgeon declared victoriously. "The tumor was completely encapsulated; we got it all. I saw some spots on her liver, so I biopsied them but they came back negative. It's probably just some old scar tissue. She'll be in recovery for a while and then we'll keep her in ICU for the night. Go home and take a break. You can come back and see her later, although she may not know you're here. She's pretty heavily sedated."

"Thank you for saving my mom's life. We are all so grateful."

"No problem. It's my pleasure. I'm glad it worked out this way. Take care, and call if you have any questions."

Since we were exhausted and couldn't see Mom for several hours, Arlyn and I left the hospital. We got the kids situated and I drove back to the hospital in the darkness of that clear evening. The hospital policy only allowed me ten minutes of visitation time, but I needed Mom to know that I was there, and I needed to be there for her. She was sleeping. I took her hand, leaned over to her face, and told her, "They got it out, Mom—all of it. It was completely encapsulated. You will be fine; don't worry!"

She grunted and groaned what I knew to be an acknowledgement.

"Get some rest. I'll be back in the morning. I love you!"

She squeezed my hand slightly to let me know she heard me.

Recovery took about ten days before she was able to go home. She's a remarkable woman—a giver, a fighter, and someone you always want to be in your corner.

Chapter Twenty-four

A Persistent Reminder

Florida was out. There were too many things that needed to be settled before the end of the year. Money was dear and couldn't be allocated to front a major trip, so it would have to wait. Several years ago in a similar situation we took a two-day trip to Baltimore where we were able to do some business and enjoy ourselves with very little expense. I started to investigate the possibilities and found a great deal in a wonderful hotel. I set up some potentially profitable meetings with a few dealers, clients, and museum curators whom I hadn't seen in quite a while. We were all looking forward to this mini-getaway.

The day before we were to leave, I was walking back to the gallery after a meeting at the bank. It was quite warm for late December so there were a lot of people on the streets. Three girls who were walking in front of me, obviously on their way back to their workplace, looked across the street to the Art Alliance and made comments of disbelief as they continued to look away and look back again. I don't know what prompted me to glance over, as I don't usually make other people's business my own, but I was drawn to look at this curious spectacle attracting their attention.

Suspended from the front of this magnificent old building was a giant rope noose. It was most likely an advertisement for an exhibition that was about to open. For me though, having lost a brother who hanged himself when I was sixteen, it shocked me as a vivid reminder of one of the darkest times in my life. After thirty something years, I have long forgiven Bruce. I have come to realize that such an act was not in anger or aimed at any of us, but was the result of what must have been an unbearable internal pain coupled with utter desperation.

Later that day, the image of the noose across the street kept presenting itself in my mind. As I was writing a letter to a client in Connecticut, I noticed his address was in Bruce Park. I was beginning to see a connection to something, but I still couldn't define it. I chalked it up to a couple of signs which would either be clarified or just go away. I should have known better.

The next day we piled the family into the Jeep after stowing the suitcases which were laden with apparel for nearly spring-like weather. We were looking forward to the promise of seventy-two degree temperatures and sunny skies for the next couple of days in Baltimore. We checked into the Harbour Court Hotel which lavished us with a huge and luxurious suite thanks to one of Arlyn's old business connections. After we deposited our belongings and made a few business calls, we walked over to the Harborplace to eat lunch. It was a glorious day; sunny and into the sixty-degree range by noon. It was only a slight bit cooler than it was in Florida where the weather was terrible that week.

Walking along the harbor, I called one of the museum curators I needed to see, and we made arrangements to meet in the next half hour. I left Arlyn with the kids to wander for a couple of hours and I walked back to the hotel to get the car to go to the museum. I met with the curator for an hour or so and felt that this had been a very productive afternoon. That evening we had dinner with a couple of clients with whom we enjoyed spending some time to review their market needs.

Later that night Arlyn and I were watching some mindless television as Howard Stern was interviewing a guest. She told of the trauma she endured as she discovered the daughter of Jerry Van Dyke after she had hanged herself. I couldn't believe my ears. I tried to block out the signal being broadcast to me, but it was like a bad dream that wouldn't stop repeating except that it kept changing faces as it continued to appear in different places. Eventually it subsided and I let it fade in my mind.

The following week I was working on a chapter of this book late one afternoon after everyone had gone home for the day. I was sitting at the computer in my office hammering away at the keyboard when I felt a tremendous thud that shook the entire building with a jolt like a small earthquake tremor. I jumped up and nervously ran out front to see whether there might be a big truck unloading a monster crate or something. The street was empty. I went up to the second floor, and then to the third...nothing anywhere. On the fourth floor, I felt a strange presence which chilled me. Normally, I would chalk it up to a one-time event but this had also occurred late one day when only Shawn and I were there. We had scoured the place and found nothing. Since Bruce had taken his life in the gallery on the upper floor, I began having very strong feelings that he was attempting to communicate with me.

There had been a similar occurrence about a year prior. It was late in the day, and I was at the computer working on another chapter of this same book, when I heard heavy footsteps coming from the second floor. I panicked, thinking there was an intruder in the building. As I approached the underside of the stairs by the storage closet, the footsteps stopped and again there was no one visible. At that time, I was more afraid than curious so I got my coat, set the alarm, locked up, and left quickly.

Alan and Mom

The week after returning from our Baltimore trip, Alan came down from New York. He was only in town for a week or so and wanted to see Mom and me just to catch up before going back. Though he left the business over ten years prior, it seemed like it was yesterday that we were working so well together, forging forward through all kinds of impossible situations. We picked up some sandwiches for lunch and were sitting around talking. The buzzer rang and in walked a pretty young woman who asked for me.

As I came out, she said, "Hi, I'm Judy. I told you I'd stop in some day. Well, I was in the neighborhood and at last had the chance." She looked very familiar but I wasn't sure I remembered her. "We met in the supermarket, remember...Judy Creed?"

"Oh, yes! Judy Creed. Forgive me. I remember you. Oh, this is my mother. Mrs. David. Mother, this is Judy."

"I was a good friend of Bruce," Judy blurted. My mother's face paled for a moment, and I wondered if mine did as well. I had forgotten that Judy and Bruce were close for a while.

Just then, Alan walked into the front of the gallery as he finished his phone call to Ronnie—another very close friend of our family whom we had adopted as our brother. He was also a large part of the same circle of Bruce's friends. This was mind-blowing. I knew then that I needed to pay attention to what was being shown to me in a most persistent fashion. I wondered what was coming next, and beyond that, what it all meant.

The next morning I awoke with a stiff neck which yielded to a headache that wouldn't quit. Was I getting physical symptoms of Bruce's pain, specifically in the area of his demise? It was becoming plausible. Recently, I had encountered six different indications related to Bruce. I was convinced of the connection, but still hadn't been able to decipher the communication. I was open to the reality that perhaps Bruce was trying to contact me for some reason. I am still unsure exactly what was happening, but I was ready to receive the next piece of the puzzle. In contrast to the fears of yesterday, I now examine with eagerness the meaning of these extraordinary events with the hope of understanding what Bruce's spirit is trying to tell me.

At the time of his death, I couldn't have been closer to anyone than I was to Bruce. I still think of him whenever I hear oldies from the mid-sixties. Sometimes the tears come, and I don't even realize why. Then, it hits me and I turn up the volume full blast. I guess some would turn it off or change stations, but tuning into it, for me, is staying with it instead of running from it. I don't know how Mom and Pop survived Bruce's death. I guess if it weren't for Alan and me, they'd have given up on life altogether. Maybe they were sufficiently united to have made it through anyhow, but I do think we were a major factor in their healing. We could never have replaced Bruce, as no one can ever take the place of another sibling. That was not our intention. But we did help bridge the awful chasm presented by his death. Needless to say, we all bore lifelong scars which are like a disease in remission—one that has no complete cure. There isn't a day that goes by that doesn't carry either a verbal or a mental allusion to him.

I'll never forget the times Bruce was there for me. One summer Friday night, three friends and I wound up in a pizza parlor in a particularly tough south Philadelphia neighborhood. Within an hour, we had teams of police there to defend us against a rather vile critter who had just broken out of jail. He was threatening us with death sentences, banging on the windows, and pointing at us. When I got home that night, Bruce was waiting for me. "I was waiting for a call from you," he greeted, "just had a feeling you were in trouble." How uncanny that he'd have known. I shared the evening's events with him, but he wasn't at all surprised. I never had to solicit Bruce's help. He would offer before I had the opportunity to open my mouth, especially if it involved a situation where asking for help would intimidate or injure my ego. He was very keen in perceiving that kind of thing, and very skillful in short circuiting it so no one would have to belittle themselves.

Bruce took me out to practice driving for days in advance of taking my driver's test after I turned sixteen. I recall the countless hours of driving through unfamiliar winding roads and expressways which I'd probably not cross again more than ten times in my lifetime. His navy blue F-85 cruised along sipping fuel so judiciously the gauge seemed like it was glued to the full marker. The V-6 engine wasn't real fast, but quick and quiet, though it emitted an almost throaty resonance when we kicked her down. The gearing was such that we needed almost no pedal pressure to maintain speed; it just floated along indefinitely.

Bruce took me for my driving test, and I used his car. When we got to the Belmont State police barracks, I was still rehearsing the questions and answers in the booklet from which the state trooper would randomly sequester five to seven of the more ambiguous questions. They were known for being tough.

I was next in line. *Oh God. I would have to get* him; *he looks mean!* The trooper nodded as he motioned me toward the car. I gulped as I shakily walked and nervously slid into the driver's seat. I buckled my seat belt, and waited until he fastened his belt. I started the engine and waited for his direction which I followed as if he were a general in the Army. I answered all of his questions quickly and correctly while driving through the course. I parallel parked, made the U turn, negotiated the left and right turns (remembering all the proper signals), came to a full stop at the stop sign, succeeded with the backup, and thought I was doing well.

I couldn't figure out why he was writing all the while but when I came to the end, he stated, "Very good. You can come back again for the driving portion anytime after twenty-four hours."

"What for?"

"You brushed the curb on your right turn." He opened the door and went on to his next victim.

Bruce got in. He knew exactly what had happened. I was so ashamed; I couldn't even look him in the face. I felt like such a total failure and I was enraged.

"We'll come back in a day or two. You'll do it; don't worry," Bruce comforted. "Those guy's snag you on the slightest infraction; it's their job."

Bruce brought me back again in two days, and I passed.

I never doubted that my brother would always be around; he was my idol. No two boys could have been closer. If I got a bad grade in school or a reprimand, I'd tell Bruce before anyone else, and that's as far as it would go. He'd tell me how to approach Mom so she wouldn't freak out. He really helped me deal with my growing pains.

I came home from high school failing math or history—I can't remember which since I was lousy in both—and I was a wreck. I never got less than a C, mostly As and Bs, so to flunk was an absolute disgrace. Bruce told me to explain it to Mom in terms she would understand. "You should tell her that you've tried your best and that you just can't make any headway, and that you didn't want to tell her because you thought you could handle it on your own," he suggested.

That was all true, so I explained it to Mom as he told me to, and it worked. She didn't get nuts. In fact, she sympathized and offered to get me a tutor.

Bruce didn't find academics of particular fascination; he was more tuned to souped up cars, rock music, and girls, and was damned good at all of them. His mechanical skills were innate, as was his charisma. He was totally and completely devoid of guile. A creation so full of love and care, he angered only when pushed beyond the limit, and mostly on the behalf of someone else. That was the essence of a sweet and handsome blue-eyed young man whose psyche grew weary of life's daily travails and ultimately pulled the plug.

Chapter Twenty-Five

Enraged for What?

The day began in typical style for a Saturday. I was up early, stumbling for a mug of strong aromatic coffee to bring me to consciousness, and then off to the gallery. We opened our doors at 9 a.m. and hoped for a client or two to venture in and make an acquisition over the course of the day. Our business is completely unpredictable and is especially so on Saturdays. It was rare for the mornings to be busy and this one was no exception.

It was approaching 1 p.m. when the phone broke the silence. It was Mom on the family line.

"Hello," I canted cheerfully.

"I'm so mad!" Mom steamed. "I had a flood in my kitchen. The dishwasher backed up and overflowed and I've been mopping water for the last hour and a half!" She was mumbling and her words were coming out like they were in slow motion.

"Mom, take it easy. Maintenance will come up and fix it. It's just water; don't worr..."

"Son of a bitch!"

"Mom, are you okay? You sound kind of funny."

"Yeah, whadeeyaa mean?"

"You just slurred your words a bit."

"I did?" she puzzled.

"Mom, stay put. I want you to stop mopping. I'll call you right back." I hung up and frantically dialed our good friend Fred Lublin, a world-renowned neurologist and reached him on his private line.

"Fred, it's Carl. I'm sorry to bother you but I think my mother may have just had a mini-stroke!" I told him what had just transpired and that her speech was slurred.

"You're probably right. It does sound like a mini-stroke. Bring her right in. I'll meet you in the emergency room."

His words cramped my stomach. I composed myself and as calmly as possible called Mom back.

"I just spoke with Fred and he wants to see you at Jefferson just as a precaution." I expected she would fight me.

"Okay. Maybe he should check me out. My arm feels kind of funny."

"Funny? how?"

"A little weak and it's kinda hard to lift it," she explained.

"I'll be right there. "

I drove straight to her apartment, picked her up and raced to the emergency room at Jefferson Hospital. I dropped her off with the triage nurse, parked the car, and ran back to meet her. Fred was already examining her as she recounted the earlier events of the day. He was very warm and calm as he told her, "Flora, you've had a very minor stroke. It's just a mini-stroke," he added assuredly.

"I knew it! I just knew it! That goddamned dishwasher!!" she fumed.

"Mom, take it easy. It's just water! Jesus, your health is more important and you need to stay calm," I commanded.

"He's right, Flora" Fred intervened. "You need to stay calm! We're going to admit you. You'll be part of an experimental drug trial. It's brand new and you are a perfect candidate." He was referring to TPA, the latest drug therapy designed to dissolve clots. It needed to be administered within a certain amount of time after a stroke in order to be effective. "You will make a full recovery and quickly at that. You may need short-term physical therapy after you are discharged."

"My grandson's bar mitzvah is a month away, will I be able to go?" She asked with a saddened face.

"Flora, I will dance with you at Brett's Bar Mitzvah; that's a promise!"

I choked back tears as her smile returned. The moment was priceless; so full of heart.

"I'll take you up on that," Mom beamed warily.

Fred got her situated in a private room and made sure the treatment got under way without delay. We were told officially that she might receive the drug itself, or a placebo as this was a double-blind study so no one could know the true identity. I knew with every fiber in my body that Fred would make certain Mom got the drug, not the placebo. We were good friends and I knew he would help my mother.

After a couple of days Mom began to show signs of significant improvement and was released with a mandatory physical therapy program that she followed to the letter. Several times a week I would drive her there and take her home after her hour of strenuous workout. Six weeks later, she was dismissed altogether with a full range of motion and use of her arm and fingers, absent of any numbness.

She did in fact have that dance with Fred at the bar mitzvah of her youngest grandson Brett. It was a moment of reverie and was one of the highlights of the entire evening.

Chapter Twenty-Six

The Unconscious Never Forgets

Mom had a minor stroke, Shawn had suffered terribly with an intestinal problem for two months, and in May, we lost Popie to a coronary. He was Arlyn's grandfather, but he raised her as a father, so his death was extremely traumatic for her. It was very hard on the kids too, for he was the only grandfather they ever knew. I had known Popie for nearly twenty-two years, and we were really close. He was an incredible man. Eighty-three years was too early to go.

The day was drawing to a close, and I was exiting the off ramp from the expressway on the way home when suddenly I felt a twinge in my chest. There was pain, but this was not like any I'd experienced before. It wasn't disabling, but it worried me. Was I going to have to endure a heart attack too? *This can't be happening to me.*

When I got home and eased into the house, I took a breath and tried to relax. I aimed for the refrigerator and grabbed for some food to sop up the caustic juices from the coffee I'd had an hour before. It seemed to help for the moment. I took a Zantac to quell the rest of what hopefully would be only a bad attack of gastric distress. God, I was feeling lousy. All I could think about was Pop. *Was this what he had for those weeks before he died? Is this going to get worse?*

Which hospital should I be rushed to? Lankenau is close; Bryn Mawr is not too far; Jefferson or Penn more comforting, but the damned traffic on the expressway would be dreadful because of the Phillies' final playoff game. Christ, what to do? I decided to chill and see how the Zantac worked. Nothing rash..not yet.

After almost half an hour I began to feel a little better. I was still worried, but my improvement gave me another perspective on the situation. I allowed for the possibility that I might not die. *I can't die, not now! My God, Brett's bar mitzvah is just weeks away! I couldn't even imagine the horror of a scenario like that. How the hell could I do that to my kid?* Whatever force is out there wouldn't dare to do that to us. It just couldn't!

I kept praying that this was just indigestion. If I died now, my family would be in shambles. Shawn and Brett would be a total mess, and likely lose their zest for life. College next year for Shawn would suddenly have little, if any appeal. I know him, he'd probably aim for the family business and try to make a go of it. With his business acumen, he'd probably be quite successful, though things in this economy have been brutal for the past few years. Somehow, I just don't see him letting the business terminate. I think he'd probably want to take the helm and see what he could do. Difficult as things would be, I'd bet on his winning over the long term.

I guess if anything did happen to me, the whole family would pull together and work the business as a team. It's nice to think so anyhow. But, if that wasn't the optimal choice, then plan B would be to sell the whole thing and cash out. I'd certainly have no objections, if that was what Arlyn and the kids wanted to do. I'd want whatever made it easiest for them. But, if there was even a trickle of desire to maintain position, I'd say go for it and give it a run for a while. They could always sell later. Anyhow, the markets will only improve with time, and they could maximize profits by utilizing a slow sell.

Through the evening, I allowed a bit of reality to seep through my self-protective veil of denial by acknowledging that Bruce had died during this week in 1965. The thought would come and go fleetingly as I accepted and refused admission to the old wound. I never was quite sure of the exact date of his death. I knew it was mid-October, but I had blocked out enough to remain in the dark about it. I sure as hell knew that it was this week, and always seemed to approach the anniversary with a mixture of casual awareness and morbid fear. After twenty eight years of this, one would think that it would get easier. It doesn't. It's akin to a limb being cut off your body. The scar and pain of loss is permanent. Oh, you manage to live your life well, but periodically you get this tremendously overwhelming reminder that brings you to your knees again.

I was still feeling lousy, so I took another Zantac and went to bed. I had talked with Arlyn, and a few tears funneled their way through my eyes, so I was at least exiting denial. Could this be the reason I was so uncentered? *Just let me live through the night and feel normal in the morning....*

Morning came, and I did feel better. Not altogether, but I sensed that if I could vent my sadness, then I could get through this thing once more. You can't force tears, it just doesn't work. I got everyone ready for the day's routine and got into the car headed for work. Howard Stern was predictable, and I knew I had feelings to get to, so I pushed in my Neil Young tape, and listened to a few cuts like "Old Man," "Till The Morning Comes," and "Southern Man." I don't know if it was the lyrics, the rhythm, or just the era from which it came, but images of my past flooded my memory banks. It was as if time had absolutely stood still. It was 1965 and everything and nothing had changed. I was sixteen years old. I was forty-four years old. It didn't matter. Age was ageless as time was timeless. Time is a device which we have created to measure our experiences, nothing more.

I cried with agonized relief. The tears were unbridled. They flowed and ebbed as they pleased, and I made no restrictions. I knew I had to feel the pain and release myself from the prison. I could no longer keep the nightmare captive. Feelings can be treasonous if abused, so the game had to end.

The weird thing was that even if I weren't consciously tuned into the date, I would still have known to the day. The unconscious never forgets...ever! It's the motherboard of the mind, a permanently etched memory filled with every single event, thought, and experience that has occurred from the moment of our existence in this world. Once and for all, I had to know Bruce's death date. I was feeling awful on the thirteenth; this year, it was a Wednesday. When I got to the gallery, I logged into my digital diary and looked back to the calendar year 1965. I couldn't believe what I saw. Wednesday, October thirteenth. Just like 1993. The numbers were identical. It freaked me out for a second, then I understood it all too well.

Chapter Twenty-Seven

Who's There?

Arlyn had grown an events management company from scratch. She used the campgrounds to host company picnics for as many as a thousand people per group. Most weekends were taken up with organizing an event or physically being on site to oversee the help and make sure everything went smoothly. Arlyn and Brett were working a picnic one Saturday and Shawn was out with his friends for the afternoon. I'd been running around the neighborhood attending to errands and decided to stop at the house to walk our Schipperke dog named Nellie. I planned to relax for a few minutes before going up to see Arlyn and Brett, but it was a hot summer day and I was in no particular hurry.

I took care of Nellie, and sat down to read a few chapters of a book. When I finished, I went into the kitchen for a cold drink. I smelled smoke from a cigarette. Now that in itself wouldn't be so unusual except for the fact that I was alone, and I don't smoke! I looked around the room and of course saw nothing. All of the windows were closed tightly so it couldn't have been coming in from outside.

"Okay, who are you?" I said aloud. I felt a wave of chill pass through me and I felt the spirit of what I thought was Arlyn's grandfather. I acknowledged the presence and was satisfied that I was simply receiving an answer to my recent request to have my guardian angel make itself known to me. Actually, I felt wonderful and couldn't wait to tell Arlyn. I knew it would please her.

About a week or so later, I was working at the computer one morning when suddenly the air around me was permeated with the smell of stale cigar smoke. We don't allow smoking of any kind in the gallery so I knew it was a spiritual message. Shawn, Eve, and Annabelle were all there at the time but I was the only one who noticed the ashen smell. It was strong enough that I don't know how they could miss it.

I called Arlyn to tell her of this strange experience, suggesting that I thought her grandfather was here. He was a cigar smoker in years past.

"Didn't your father smoke cigars?" Arlyn's response moved me.

"Yeah, he did, after he quit smoking cigarettes."

"Well, there you are. Maybe you had the identity wrong when you were greeted with the cigarette smoke in the house last week. You're just getting a second message to wake you up since you missed the first one."

"You're probably right," I agreed. "Pop is the one visiting me."

Some days the pain of Pop's absence is as fresh as it was that first day of August, back in 1973 when I had barely put my pieces back together from the ever devastating loss of my brother. In retrospect, I don't know how I got through it. I miss Pop, and when I look at our two boys, I pray they never know such pain. I'd do anything to spare them.

Chapter Twenty-Eight

The Next Generation of Art Dealers

The years sped by way too quickly. Bar mitzvahs were performed and celebrated in warm, loving style with an elegant flair. Driving tests were studied for and passed, licenses were earned. Teenage years were survived, high school graduations were over, and college admissions were taken care of. Girlfriends, first loves, and heartbreaks, all took place in the course of tradition. Shawn and Brett grew into wonderful men of whom we are exceptionally proud. They are both kind, caring, compassionate, handsome beings with whom we have been very blessed.

Shawn graduated high school in 1994. Afterward, he attended a local campus of Penn State University for a semester. College was of little interest to him. He knew what he wanted at an early age—to come into the family business. He had worked summers and holidays with me for the past three years, and developed a wonderful sense of the business. Brett joined us two summers ago, and as a threesome, we work beautifully together. He also has an innate sense of things in the gallery. We share business approaches to a multitude of situations on a daily basis, and the three of us arrive at the best solutions. It is a fantastically enriching experience to spend time with them. At the end of each summer, I dreaded seeing the school term start again because I sadden at the thought of returning to the gallery without my boys. Schooling does come first, but that doesn't mean a father can't have aspirations and hopes for both of his sons to come into the business. I was thrilled when Shawn brought it up one day.

"Dad, I have a question for you."

"Shoot." I allowed, not thinking much of it.

"I hate college; it's not for me. I know what I want to do with my life and I think I deserve a chance." He paused. I stayed silent, although I had a pretty accurate idea of where he was going with this sales pitch.

"And...." I pushed.

"I want to come in to the business and really learn it. I want to be an art dealer," he continued. "I know I'll be good at it. I don't want to waste four years at school and then start doing what I knew all along I wanted to do. That'd be a complete waste of time.......and money." He was serious. "If I am going to wind up in the business anyhow, why can't I start now? I'll do all the grunt work, whatever needs to be done, I don't care. Pay me what you will, just so I have enough to live until I can earn my own way." He paused........"I won't disappoint you, I promise."

"Let me talk with your mother and I'll give you an answer tomorrow."

"Thanks, Dad. I really appreciate it."

"No problem."

Shawn's argument was solid. It would be hard to refute such sound and genuine logic.

Arlyn and I concurred that Shawn should be given the opportunity to face his future like a kid who gets scouted by a pro ball team and takes the plunge. We assured him that coming in to the business was not going to be a cakewalk and that he'd have to earn his stripes just like I did. Nothing would be given without responsibility just because his last name was David.

Teaching Shawn the family business reminded me of my first art deal. January of 1971 was cold and Pop and I were on our way to make a call to the widowed ex-girlfriend of the Philadelphia artist, Fred Wagner. She lived along the track-laden cobblestoned path of the trolleys in Chestnut Hill and had telephoned us that morning to say that she wanted to sell all the works by Wagner in her possession. Pop told her we'd be there around seven o'clock that evening.

"This one is yours," he exclaimed calmly as we were pulling up to the brownstone nestled between the shops of the neighborhood.

"What?" I gasped. "What d'ya mean this one's mine?"

"Just what I said, this deal is all yours. You can handle it, I have every confidence."

"Great, I don't even know what there is here and I'm supposed to make the call and tell her what we'll pay for this stuff?"

"Yep."

"Oh terrific," I threw back with contempt. "Thanks a whole lot!"

"C'mon, you can do this. Do you think I'd let you embarrass me?" he taunted.

Now I had no choice but to take the challenge and make this a success. Otherwise, I'd not only disappoint him, but I'd look like an idiot and possibly alienate a client and lose the deal altogether. I'd have to evaluate the group of works, decide what they were worth in aggregate in the long run, ballpark the costs of preparing them for market and account for the cost in the interim. All the while I had to be fair to the seller and make sure she was happy, not insulted but not getting the better of the deal. Quite a ball of twine to unravel.

"Okay, I'll do it but if I screw this up it's your fault."

He laughed as his eyes shot through me. "Don't you dare!"

We left the warm comfort of the station wagon and walked up the three uneven concrete steps to her street side row house with the green and white striped awning. Pop rang the bronze door bell and a moment later a lovely gray-haired lady greeted us as we exchanged pleasantries. She waved us inside.

On the floor were several boxes of oil paintings and watercolors neatly arranged in size order. I was dying to get a look at the paintings they held.

"Excuse me, may I take a look through them?" I asked.

"Please," she smiled.

I examined each one making a mental note as to the long distance value and the quick sell so I would have a perspective as to best and worst case scenario. There were beautiful Impressionist panels of harbor scenes in Philadelphia and New York, spring and winter landscapes, and a host of watercolors of similar subject.

After about fifteen minutes I said, "Do you want to sell these in their entirety as a group?"

"Yes, I need the money and I'm moving."

"Okay. I am willing to buy the lot for $X,000. I have to put a lot more money into them to make them salable. If that is agreeable, I'll write you a check." I held my breath trying not to be arrogant or appear uncertain.

Her response was quick. "I think that's fair, after all you do have to make money too," she acknowledged. "We have a deal."

"Thank you for understanding." I was delighted as the beads of sweat began to evaporate.

I wrote her a check and shook her hand with thanks and began to take the group of boxes out to the car and load them into the cargo area. Several trips later we were on the way home and Pop, after a minute of deafening silence spoke, "That was beautiful. You handled yourself like a gentleman."

"Thanks." I waited anxiously to see if he thought I overpaid.

"And," he paused, " you bought that lot for an amazing price. We will do very, very well." Whew, I made the cut. Now I could relax. "I'm really proud of you," he added. "That must have been really difficult, being the first deal and going in cold. You are going to be a great art dealer, I have no doubts." He put his arm around my shoulder and squeezed and then patted me on the back of my head.

"I love you, Pop."

"I love you, too!"

Shawn learned as he went and I gave him as many survival tools as I could impart to him. He quickly became a great dealer with a real aptitude for the art business. He has a great eye and is well suited to this career path. He has done us proud and has expanded the business with an impressive list of his own clients.

Chapter Twenty-Nine

Twin Engines

Our dear friends Danny and Eileen invited us to spend a week with them in a villa they booked in St. Barth so we jumped at this extraordinary opportunity. We had to take a roundabout route to get there. After a day-long sojourn from Philadelphia to San Juan, with a two-hour layover, followed by a lousy turbulent flight to St. Maarten in an very crowded, hot, and noisy ATR 72, we arrived by taxi, a might weary, to a marvelous boutique hotel in St. Maarten. We planned to stay in St. Maarten for one night and then take the 2:40 island hopper to St. Barth to meet them the following day.

We were welcomed in St. Maarten by a refreshing rum punch and several high recommendations for dinner. We checked into the beachside suite, the only room available that night, changed into sandals and strolled up the darkening beach to the lull of the gently lapping waves for a mile or so. We found Le California, a French bistro on the beach, and wandered inside.

The menu was an elegant beckoning array of French delights; extensive, enticing, and affordable. They offered a one-to-one exchange against the euro for cash, instead of the 1:1.27 prevailing rate. It was wonderfully romantic and sensually saturating in every way. After we finished our gastronomic treat, we enjoyed the traditional offering of a shot of banana vanilla rum. After dinner we walked back through the streets of Grand Case, a section of St. Maarten, which is home to some great upscale French restaurants, quaint boutique shops, art galleries, and street vendors interspersed with a plethora of poverty-laden dwellings. After waiting out a short-lived tropical deluge, we traversed the flooded dirt street. Following our cultural tour, we walked back to Le Petit Hotel where our suite overlooked the sea, with Anguilla twinkling in the distance across the seven miles of adjacent water.

A few hours later the rains returned with a vengeance. It seemed like a monsoon and it didn't let up for a minute all night. It was still coming down relentlessly the next morning and we were uncertain as to whether we'd be able to fly out to St. Barth even later in the afternoon. The airport had been closed for hours, all flights were cancelled and we made back up reservations for another room at the sister hotel in the hills, just in case. At about noon it seemed to lighten up a bit and we were taxied to the airport with the hopes of finding a window in the weather just long enough to make the quarter-hour crossing to the revered resort island. The airport was a zoo with everyone trying to reschedule their flights, but we managed to check our baggage and get our seats counted and waited for the 2:40 flight to be called. At three o'clock we were hailed to board and walked a couple of blocks to get to our airplane as we passed the general and private aircraft chocked in their temporary homes.

It had been decades since I had flown in a twin-engine airplane.

The Winair 22 seat transport was a Dehavilland Twin Otter high wing bird that had made hundreds if not thousands of these hops across the islands. Painted white and blue with yellow highlights, she was tinged with exhaust stains behind the engine cowlings, and darkened by the sooty residue. I did my own visual and mental walk around. It was habit, I couldn't help myself; it was unconscious behavior; a vestige from the old days. We climbed up the four-step asphalt-coated aft steps holding onto the thickly-braided flexing cable grips and with lowered heads we entered this veteran people mover to the front row. We sat down and buckled ourselves in. I needed to sit where I had a clear view into the cockpit so I could read the instruments and watch with imagined companionship as I flew right seat. The altimeter was set to 200 feet as the US Air pilot turned over the right engine. She began to rotate with windmill-like precision as a puff of dark smoke blew out the exhaust while the slowly turning individual blades increased momentum and melded into a single quickening circle. The vibration made its way through the window into the cabin and fell into the seat. A minute or two after, the left engine awoke with a whining as its four-bladed propeller began to rotate rhythmically as she spun up to meet the synchrony of right motor.

Both cockpit doors were pulled closed and locked, the radios squawked and the traditional airline greetings were muffled into the cabin, first in English, then French, as we began to taxi out to the single runway of the airport. The rain had stopped and the visibility was getting better by the minute. We taxied further to the apron and held short while the engines were run up and gauges were checked. Switches were flipped, trims adjusted, frequencies set, and a myriad of finite adjustments were set as required for our departure. A small single engine aircraft landed and turned off the runway as we lined up to take off. The pilot pushed both overhead throttles gently forward to their limits. We felt the thrust pin us to our seatbacks as forward motion mounted very quickly and lifted us off the ground with great stability and a loftiness that only small propeller-driven planes can deliver. As the runway diminished behind us, we pulled over the mountain banking toward the harbor beneath us so richly colored with the aqua blue blanket that enveloped the sailboats and luxury yachts docked there. As I surmised, we climbed to a 1,500-foot cruise for the short trip and within another minute we locked in and straightened our course. There were rain showers scattered to the left and there was a clearing to the right. I eyeballed the artificial horizon: exhaust gas temperature gauges, mixture indicators, turn and bank, airspeed, fuel flow meter, radios, and a mass of other instruments in the cluster. We flew over an azure sea interrupted by an occasional catamaran or Italian yacht. The air was exceptionally smooth but for an infrequent nudge that served as a reminder not to get too comfortable. Visibility was at about twenty miles and improving as St. Barth's L-shaped profile revealed itself to our left. The red- and orange-roofed villas jutted from the sides of the mountains. The rugged landscape was magnificent. Tiny roads wound up and down and twisted their way in and out of the lush, foliated hills growing out of this once volcanic edifice into such splendor.

In a few more minutes we would be making our approach into the notorious runway obscured from sight by the mountain that bordered it and necessitated a steep and precipitous drop to the airport below. All commercial pilots are required to have thousands of hours of experience and certification before attempting this airport. The winds had reversed so we would be making our final approach from the beach on the other side. Turning, we would come straight in with full flaps and pitches flat as our rpms increased but with airspeed blowing off. We were about 100 feet over the beach and about 110 knots as beachgoers waved beneath us from the sparkling sapphire water. I'd done this dozens of times on the simulator. It was thrilling to actually make this approach in an airplane. I felt as if I'd flown this bird myself. We glided down to a very graceful, nearly imperceptible touchdown as thrusts reversed for about ten seconds before we turned off the runway to the small building that housed the customs and baggage departments.

The engines spun to a halt and the aft door opened for us to deplane. Row by row everyone got up and stepped down onto the laddered door to the ground in St. Barth. The smells, the sounds, the characteristics, the feelings, the memories were all so vivid in their return. So many years gone by and yet in an instant the distance was bridged as if time was stilled, brought to a grinding halt by the reins of a re-enactment. Are we just a record of physical, mental, spiritual, and emotional timeless experiences? A vault of layers of events turned into memory and compressed into instant recall at the whim of a thought or suggestion.

Chapter Thirty

College Days Are Here Again

In 1999, Brett was in his senior year of high school when he visited a good friend at Penn State's main campus. He came back firmly stating that he would spend the next four years there. And so he did, all the while garnering a myriad of honors and learning how to survive on his own. Having my son in college reminded me of my own college days at Oglethorpe University in Atlanta, Georgia.

Mom and I flew to Atlanta that July to have a look around. We rented a car and followed the map until we found the place about forty-five minutes northeast of the airport. We parked and walked into the ivy-covered façade of what was obviously the administration building and met the dean who seemed very affable. Maybe this wouldn't be so bad after all. We left his office with full assurance that both the academics and social life would far surpass any which I had yet experienced.

We traversed the entire campus, which wasn't huge, but on a fire-searing day, it was unbearably hot in the high 90's and as humid as a dragon's breath. We were deep in the midst of the wooded path between the offices and the boy's dorms, when Mom froze dead in her tracks and clenched my arm.

Pointing, she said, "That's a rattlesnake ahead on the walkway."

"Yep, sure is," I feigned bravery. A sudden chill vanquished the heat of that day and made it feel like the approach of winter. My body had become filled with electricity and fear. We gave it the due respect it deserved, and then wasted no time in getting to our destination. After that, we never lifted our eyes from the ground in front of us.

Next, we surveyed the school. We eyeballed the dorms and breezed through one of them so I could glimpse my new surroundings. This being late May, it had been abandoned for the summer, so no one was there. The place had a stillness akin to a distant desert, yet it beckoned with friendship and warmth. I was convinced that we had made the proper choice. As I walked down the stairs and went outside I felt a twinge of excitement. I knew this would be the beginning of a phenomenal chapter in my life.

The summer flew as it surrendered swiftly to September. The evenings began to take on a chill that let us know the dramatic heat had all but burned out. The leaves were yellowing and some were tinted toward a sunset. The grass wasn't growing wildly anymore and the days had noticeably shortened. Darkness set in by 7:30 and the air smelled pungently crisp with the awakenings of Autumn. The aroma bore reminiscence of that "back to school" time which came like clockwork with each ever so rapidly passing summer.

It was time to pack clothes for summer, fall, and winter. Autumn would be delayed at least another month in Atlanta, and I had no idea how severe the winters would be there. Being that far to the south, it was reputed that snow didn't exist, but that it got windy and quite cold from December to March. They neglected to tell me about the disgusting rivers of red mud which blanketed every inch of ground when it rained for six and seven days in a row. The soil was predominantly red clay and when it softened it was like quicksand engulfing its victims from the boots up! So, the boots I packed because I thought they were "tough" looking served a practical application.

I took my clock radio, razor, newly-opened checkbook, camera, little heating coil for my mug to boil water for tea and soup, hair brush, toiletries, pillow, sheets, blanket, and everything else I could cram into the trunk and backseat of my two-door, green '67 Cutlass Supreme. I was dreading the next morning. Leaving home was difficult enough, but saying goodbye to Mom and Pop would be too painful to bear. I didn't want to cry in front of them because I knew it must be equally horrific for them. I hugged and kissed them both and gave them assurance that Alan and I would be careful driving and that we would call as soon as we stopped at a motel at day's end. Cellular telephones hadn't been invented at the time. I walked slowly to the car, tossed a couple of last minute items into the back, and wiped my eyes pretending to have rubbed them.

I popped into the driver's seat. "Ready?"

"Yeah, let's go-it's almost 9:30," Alan urged.

And off we went leaving Mom and Pop standing arm in arm in the window of the dining room, waving with encouragement. God, I loved them so much. I was going to miss them dreadfully, even though they were flying down in just five days.

The drive was exciting. I'd never been so far south on my own. We cleared Delaware, then Maryland, and Virginia. We continued to drive hard until about four that afternoon when we were into North Carolina. We were well past the point of being silly and decided that if we stopped, we could still catch a swim. The day was still close to ninety degrees, and ripe with mosquitoes, so we picked out a motel from our Keystone AAA Road Guide, pulled slightly off the main drag, and checked in. We backed the car almost directly up to the door to our room so nobody could get by it, or near the trunk handle. We couldn't get to some of the overnight gear we needed, but the car had my life's accumulations in it and was worth securing—even to the point of sacrifice.

Watching the gas gauge go from full to empty and then play the "bet we can go another fifty miles before we run dry" game had made us crazy. We had to unwind a while. We chose to swim and bake in the last hours of the sun before eating dinner. But first, I called Mom and Pop to let them know we were safe and sound.

After the sun descended into the distant trees, we got dressed and drove into town for dinner. We found a local eatery that promised good ole Southern cookin' where we gorged ourselves on hot crispy fried chicken, sweet corn on the cob, grits with red eye gravy, and sweet apple cobbler for dessert. With our newly donned deep southern accents, we'd never have been spotted as Yankees. We were so stuffed we could hardly move, but we managed to lift ourselves and make it to the car. We drove back to the motel, watched TV for a bit, and nodded off until sunrise.

The next day, we were off to South Carolina and into Georgia. We stopped briefly to inhale some cheeseburgers, fries, and iced tea, and laugh convulsively as we each staged our own interpretation of a southern drawl. To the southerner, the northerner talks too fast and funny and has to have everything done immediately or he cries! To the northerner, the southerner has a weird and sloppy speech pattern which takes too long to drag out of him. You want to give him clues to help him finish his sentences, and after four hours of two clever humorists conversing and looking at one another in close quarters, comic relief became spontaneous and explosive. The people around us would likely have locked us up if we didn't leave, but I don't think they realized until we were long gone that they were the subject of our amusement.

Several hours later, thoroughly exhausted, we rolled into Atlanta and drove directly to the downtown Regency Hyatt, which was then the newest and most exciting place to be. We checked in and luxuriated in this twentieth century architectural monument with glass elevators and inward facing balconies that overlooked the lobby from as high as thirty stories. Each one dripped plants that cascaded into a lattice work from floor to floor. It was spectacular. The elevators and fixtures were accented with a myriad of tiny white lights offering non-stop sparkle and glitz. Music played softly while people communicated in a harmonious lull somewhere below.

That night we ate at Hugo's, their best restaurant, ordered their largest and most succulent prime rib dinner. What the hell, after the next couple of days, I'd be eating institutional garbage, so I thought the extravagant send off was well deserved.

The next day was check-in at school. We drove to the campus, which was northeast of downtown, parked in the lot adjacent to my assigned dormitory, and began to unload the contents of the car. I met my roommates—one from Lancaster, Pennsylvania, another from Florida, and another from Georgia—a nice cross-section. The rooms were hardly elegant, but they were livable.

Mom and Pop were due in shortly, so we hung around to kill time before going to the nearby DeKalb Peachtree Airport in Chamblee—a busy general aviation field—to meet them. They hadn't arrived, so we watched and waited until finally we saw the glitter of a distant Aztec clad in white with red and black design. A few instants later they glided down to earth, parked, and deplaned. I ran over to them, brimming with excitement. We unloaded their bags and put them into my car and drove to the hotel.

We took a ride out to the campus early the next morning so Pop could see the school, meet the administrative brass, and say, "You'll take care of my boy, right?" I was sort of embarrassed, but just as flattered and secure in knowing that I would be granted immediate credibility. I was extremely well received by the president and the dean of the school, and was formally invited to see them if I had any complaints or problems anywhere along the line. Pop's power was stunningly impressive. College kids are supposed to be thwarted and intimidated by their old man's strength and wisdom. I must have been the exception. I loved it! It thrilled me to watch his mere presence take over a room full of high-powered people as he would walk through a door to greetings of reverence and handshakes that offered everything from friendship to financial and political connections. I really wondered if I would ever draw such worship or inspire such awe, but I hoped to set the tone and write the script for my life instead of acting in it at someone else's direction.

Adulthood was snuffing out my youth at a frenzied pace depriving my carefree nature with a relentless fury. Suddenly, I was confronted with responsibility. There could be no letdowns, no retreats, no failures. My folks had set me up in style and I had to come through for them and for myself as well. This two-year stretch would be my private proving grounds. I had to fare it on my own and turn in top scores.

After an intimate dinner at the Coach and Six, one of Atlanta's finest, I stayed with my parents that night, and drove them and Alan back to the airport the next morning. Hugs and kisses exchanged and I waited until they took off before I left. Suddenly, I felt alone as if I were about to perform live on stage in a concert with thousands of strange and unfamiliar eyes fixed upon me. I was a stranger in a foreign land. How odd to have such total control and feel powerless at once.

I looked around pensively through the landscape around me as my feet directed me back to the car. The gleaming green '67 Cutlass Supreme beckoned with excitement as if to say, "C'mon, we're in for a great time. No one to tell us when to go to sleep, or where not to go, or what not to do! There's a whole world out there filled with undiscovered treasure and folly, just waiting for us to find it." I kicked the pebbles out of my way, climbed in, and headed back to school. "Aw, what the hell, how bad could it be? Let's get on with the show!"

I don't know whether I was pirating my father's style or trying to impress him, undoubtedly a bit of both. I was young, ambitious, hungry, and very eager to please him. One day I caught a notice on a dormitory bulletin board that was advertising a very attractive job solicitation: "Chemical Company Sales Position Available - 50% Commission Call Now." With a payoff like that, the work was either brutally difficult or impossible. I was filled with excitement and hoped desperately that no one else had seen this outlandish proposal on the wall. I knew they must have been tacked to every ad board in the college and were too numerous to remove. What the hell, most of the crew at that school would've been too busy structuring their leisure activities to have been interested anyway, so maybe I stood a real chance to land the job. I ran to my room with ad in hand a grabbed the phone to call the guy.

"I'm Carl David," I said in a very serious voice. "I saw your ad on the bulletin in board at Oglethorpe."

"Are you willing to work hard, sell cold, and demonstrate your sales experience?" Replied a male voice.

"Yes," I explained my years of selling anything that crossed my path. I was so convincing that I sold him on my credentials and landed the job, which consisted of vending only one product: an all-purpose, super-powered, industrial-strength cleaning solution. I went to see him at his office where I was briefed in about twenty minutes. I stopped by the dorm to don the required jacket, tie, and dress pants, grabbed my briefcase, and set out to make some fast money.

I walked right into a restaurant and said, "Show me the grease and grime that nothing will touch." The manager led me to a spot near the machinery that looked weathered and relentless. "No problem," I smiled defiantly, "Watch this!"

I didn't stop to rehearse or pray; I had seen this cleaner do wonders in my twenty-minute demonstration training, and even I was confident that we could purify sewers with it. I was still pleasantly amazed and relieved when the metal beneath the spot began to gleam its path with sparkling voracity as I lifted the chemical-laden cloth from the machine. "Your problem is history," I rejoiced! "How much do you need? The more you buy now, the better the price!"

I sold him a few 55-gallon drums and procured a promise of re-order and also got leads and referrals to a couple more chain restaurants. I knew then and there that I had promise and that I was going to go places! I would've closed a real sweet deal with Frito Lay, whose operation was then headquartered in Atlanta, but the product wasn't FDA-certified and approved and they wouldn't touch it. I tried anyhow, but to no avail.

I walked into a tire outfit who would have bought anything that would've removed their fossilized treads from the floor in the showroom. Nothing short of dynamite would release those things, but I was young and determined, and just as naïve. I was blindly convinced that "my" product was invincible; the ultimate solution!

"Okay fellas," I boasted proudly, "Here goes nothing!"

I scrubbed and poured it on, and on, and on. It only seemed to accentuate the very thing I was trying desperately to eradicate, and my face was turning more ashen by the minute. I felt the color draining as all eyes were upon me with that penetrating look of an enemy who had set an invisible trap into which I walked so nonchalantly. I was wounded; my ego fractured as I heard the chuckling above me.

Glowing with embarrassment, I put my stuff away in very quick and disorganized fashion, got up, and sheepishly apologized, "Sorry guys, I would have sworn it'd work."

"No one has ever been able to get rid of those tire tracks! You aren't the first to attempt it, probably won't be the last!"

It was wonderful to take consolation in the fact that everyone lost in this game. It didn't make me feel like celebrating, but I guess some things are best left alone.

Life struggled on through the next weeks with piles of homework and studies and socializing in between. Soon, I was into the full swing of things aware that this place was going to bring full term success. November burst into color and everyone donned their sweatshirts and coats.

My telephone rang as I was half way out the door one day. All phone calls were exciting and I never knew who it might be on the other end. I ran back in and picked it up.

"Hello?"

"Hey Tad! We're flying down with some real food tomorrow. You interested?"

"Interested?" I salivated, "God, I'd kill for real food! You really coming down?"

"Yep!" he stated affirmatively. I could hear him smiling ear to ear. His excitement was hardly able to be contained. "Got to see an important client who has a couple of great Cassatt pastels and a Theodore Robinson painting of a girl on a New England hillside under a parasol. They say they'll consider selling if the monies are right, so I assured them that we'd make them very happy!"

"That's incredible! I'll meet you at the Chamblee airport," I replied with eagerness. "Just give me a time."

"Meet us at noon and we'll be there...guaranteed! Hey, kid!"

"Yeah?"

"You mean 'Yes' you meathead! Jesus, I send you all the way down there to learn and you still don't talk right."

I laughed. "Hey, Pop. What did you want to ask me?"

"Is there anything you want us to bring down for you?"

"Yeah, speech lessons!" He roared with laughter. "Seriously though, don't call me 'Meathead' or 'Tad' in front of my friends. Do me that small favor. You know it drives me crazy. Okay?"

"Sure thing!" he agreed.

"Hey, Pop, I love you...hurry up, I miss you!"

"I love you too!" he replied warmly.

"See you tomorrow."

I couldn't wait to pass the next twenty-four hours. What a shot in the arm. I was about to receive a brief but heavenly encounter in the morning. I swept, cleaned, folded and hung up clothes, and prepared the dorm to make it generally presentable.

I was up at six o'clock the next morning. It was a crisp day showing a gorgeous cloudless blue sky with a light chilling breeze and a forecast high expected in the mid 50s. I showered, got dressed, and consumed a quick breakfast. I told my roommates of the impending visit before I disappeared. I also told them of the possibility of some smuggled in home-cooked food and to keep their mouths shut if they wanted some! If the word got out I'd have had more friends than I could ever know in a normal lifetime.

I left for the airport at about eleven o'clock, got there at 11:15, parked and sat in wait, facing the runway. I got out and paced around the front of the car, and sat on the hood. The warmth of the green glistening metal underneath me felt good. Closing in on 11:30, I noticed a distant glitter with a chorus of strobe lights which had to be them. As the airplane approached, I watched in awe as Pop maneuvered the Aztec to a gentle float to the ground. Damn, he was good! I could hardly believe how facile he was with it. I knew I'd never be the pilot of such finesse. They rolled to a stop, taxied away from the runway, and parked on the grassy area nearby. I jumped onto the wing by the cabin, stepping gingerly on the black step area, and treaded judiciously. The door latch clicked loudly as it released. I grabbed the handle and opened the jar with a twist and a warm welcome.

It was good to see them. Mom looked pretty relaxed and things appeared well. Pop looked content in his rugged Levi's and dark glasses. They got out, stretched, and opened the luggage door. I could smell the intoxicating God-like aroma of the brisket and potatoes. Mom had made a feast with all the trimmings. The meat was still warm and fork-tender. The potatoes were browned and light as a feather, and a rich dark gravy embraced everything within its touch. The problem which confronted me was, how to smuggle this stuff into the dorm. The fragrance was a dead giveaway!

After we stowed the stuff, we went to visit the clients who had the paintings. I was breathless when I saw them, and was even more impressed with the way Pop handled the situation. After about forty minutes of very convincing conversation, we walked out with even more treasure than had been disclosed over the telephone. They were delighted beyond their own expectations, and we were politely grateful for their hospitality and cooperation in this matter. We assured them that no one would ever know exactly where these paintings had come from, and that great discretion would be exercised in their sale. Pop had just spent a very substantial amount of money for this cargo, but he was brimming with confidence and smiled all the way back to the airplane. He was already planning his marketing strategy and had only to decide which of his most serious clients to interest in these very important paintings.

Those memories are sweet. Long after they took off that day to return home, the sumptuous feast lingered on as we savored it for the next few days. The foil wrapped package diminished by the hour. We stowed it on the roof ledge outside our window, where it was cold and safe from all but bird and beast.

It was those special touches that enriched my life. I remember people asking me throughout my childhood of whether or not we were rich. Still today folks say, "You've always had money" or "We know you're rich." People are generally so consumed by monetary significance that they miss the real essence of life. Sure we were comfortable and never really wanted for much, but that would have been meaningless had it been the only consideration in our lives. My father worked with an enormous appetite for success. He was never a quitter and never assumed he was the only game in town; even though that was true enough! He worked demonically for what he earned. His insight and foresight was razor sharp, and he possessed an uncanny knack for predicting trends yet to be born. He often second guessed the future in his business. He'd always had a raging love affair with paintings and longed for years to convert the family's antique shop to a first-rate art gallery. The resistance from his father was strong but Pop slowly dissipated it by repeatedly scoring stunning victories with sales of paintings which he had purchased with his own funds. This transition was somewhat of an upheaval for my grandfather (David David) who knew early American furniture as expertly as he knew his own name. The man's knowledge and intellectual character was nearly encyclopedic, but he was dismayed at his son's drifting interest toward paintings. I think he viewed it as a disloyalty, but his suspicions were totally unfounded. Pop had not lost an ounce of love for the antiquities. If anything he grew to understand and respect the overall mechanism of how the objects and the old paintings were married. All of these pieces played a dramatic and intertwined role in history. When we were taken through museums Pop didn't just tell us about the paintings, he gave us the complete package: furniture, tapestries, objects of vertu, silver, jewelry, sculpture, and paintings. Of course my interest today is in paintings, but I have high regard and appreciation for all the aspects of my heritage.

Chapter Thirty-One

Brett Enters the Family Business

Brett graduated from the Smeal School of Business with honors and was eager to go corporate and apply his newfound knowledge. For the next year, he worked for a major money management firm in downtown Philadelphia and decided that wasn't for him. One day, he came to me and said, "Hey Pop, got a minute? I need to ask you a question." He sounded serious.

"Sure. What's on your mind?" I mused.

Clearing his throat, he began. "Listen, I am really appreciative for the four years you and Mom gave me at Penn State. I really learned a lot and had an amazing time. The problem is I hate working corporate. It's so boring to just crunch numbers all day. It's not at all what I expected." Wringing his hands uncomfortably, he paused. I had a hunch what was coming next. "Uh, can I come into the business with you?" He looked at me, eyes praying, "I'll work hard, do all the grunt work, whatever you need. The only thing I ask is that you teach me. I want to be a dealer. I've grown up with art. I love it, I just need to learn the business. I'll be good at it. I know I will, promise."

Not surprised, but secretly jumping up and down with excitement, I told him, "Let me discuss this with Mom and I'll let you know after we speak."

"Thanks, Pop, it really means a lot. I want to get started with my life. I feel like I'm stuck."

I spoke with Arlyn at length and we agreed that he should be given a chance so the next day, I found him and said, "Brett, Mom and I discussed your coming into the business."

He looked with unease, "And.....?"

"And, we agreed that you deserve a chance but just like we told Shawn when he wanted to come in, you don't get all the benefits just because your last name is David. You have to earn them. And you will work your tail off." I paused to read him. "This is a very difficult business and not for the faint of heart. There are no set hours; we work around the clock when we have to. Often money is tight and we're fully invested in the inventory so sometimes you may not even get a paycheck. Can you live with that? It's blood and guts around here but it's ours for better or worse."

"Sure Pop, I know that. I just need enough money to live."

"Okay then, you're in. Welcome aboard. It's a pleasure to have you with us." I smiled. He wrapped me in a huge hug of gratitude.

Wow, both sons in the family business! A dream come true! I'm not sure who was more excited, Brett or me.

Mentoring my sons in the art business, has brought back many memories of the training my Pop gave to me. I remember the Frieseke deal vividly. Arlyn and I had been married but a few months and it was a lazy Sunday morning when the telephone beckoned. I picked it up to hear Pop's cheery, authoritative voice on the other end.

"Pick me up in half an hour. We're going to Atlantic City,"

he announced. "We just bought a major mural by Frederick Carl Frieseke from the Shelburne Hotel and we need to get it out of there quickly."

There was an air of urgency, but I wasn't in the mood for work. "C'mon Pop, it's Sunday. Can't we do it tomorrow?"

"Do you want to be an art dealer or not?" He was not joking. He was not asking, but telling me what would be done.

With a smack of reality I told him, "I'll be there in thirty minutes."

I could hear his smile as he hung up the telephone. I told Arlyn what had just transpired.

"I have to go and help Pop. I am sorry for ruining the day."

"Go" she said with a smile. "Its business; your dad needs you, and that's where you need to be. I'll be here. Call me when you can. I love you."

"I love you too."

I was at Dad's building in twenty minutes. He was waiting downstairs at the door under the marquis, expecting me to be early. I knew better than to just be on time; that wouldn't have been good enough. He jumped into my car and we sped away as he filled me in on the details of the deal.

"Sonny is meeting us there with his conservation crew. The mural we just bought is by Frederick Carl Frieseke, who was commissioned in 1906 by Rodman Wanamaker to paint it in France, and then bring it to America. It was to be cut and placed around the Rotunda Dining Room that overlooks the ocean. We have to get the mural out of there before they demolish the hotel. And, we've got to take them away fast before the owners realize what they've sold and renege on the deal. These are going to be worth a fortune someday; they're literally one of a kind—super rare. They have incredible literary references and are in fairly good condition; especially for mural paintings."

216

Shelburne Hotel

Shelburne Hotel

I clearly understood the urgency. We raced on and just shy of an hour later we were at the doors of the grand old dame, the Shelburne Hotel. There she stood, gloriously proud of her heritage, showing off her magnificent façade which for decades had defied forces of nature and changes in time. As we entered the hotel, we were guided by the general manager into the dining room where our treasure lay hidden behind the floor-length, deep claret-colored velvet drapes. People were eating lunch. Silverware clanged, glasses pinged, and plates echoed as the waiters set them down on silver chargers. It was business as usual in the waning days of the life of this elegantly attired dining room housed in a great historic building which was soon to meet its sad, untimely end.

The mural was glued onto the walls so we would have to face it with the proper solvents and rice paper and then extract it with surgical precision. The length was way over one hundred linear feet. There were seven sections of magnificent scenes of women and children on the beach. Times of elegance, charm, and reverie depicted in these five-foot high Belle Époque panoramic views of life as it was in 1906 gave the impression of a carefree, fun-filled era.

We were able to work nearly incognito with our conservation experts as we very delicately prepared the paintings and very slowly and painstakingly removed them, inch by inch, one by one, and very carefully rolled them up for transport to New York where Sonny's conservation facility was located. He was a master conservator who knew when he could go farther and when to stop. He could see below the surface pigments and knew intuitively the extent of the possibilities in every situation. He was simply the best, being both a forensic scientist and an artist. Pop set him up in business many years ago when he was in the unhappy employ of another conservation studio in New York. He begged my father to help him set up his own shop. Sonny found a small but adequate location to set up his restoration studio and Pop funded him and fed him a steady stream of work while he grew the business as other outside work would filter through. In subsequent years, Sonny moved twice to larger spaces as his business had outgrown the existing location.

The fumes from our solvents were ghastly and gave pause as we watched with disbelief and hysterical laughter while the diners didn't miss a beat. Olfactory senses would have to be numb not to acknowledge the presence of such overwhelming chemical vapors.

As it turned out, this mural by Frieseke, a major American Impressionist painter whose star would shine brightly in years to follow, was the only remaining one in existence. Three of the paintings were nearly five feet in length while the four largest paintings each reached from twelve to seventeen feet. All were five feet in height. What a coup to rescue such an important piece of history.

Frieseke Summer's Glory

Frieseke After the Swim

After endless and arduous hours of painstaking efforts, we had completed the preparation, extraction, and rolling up of the seven paintings. It was late evening; all of the people had gone home except for security and the general manager. We pulled our station wagon around and loaded up the carefully camouflaged rolls which would then be transferred to a waiting truck for immediate transport to New York under cover of darkness. Sonny would begin work on the smaller paintings first. One at a time, it would be a monumental endeavor. Every other project in his workshop would have to be delayed so we would need to fund him in the interim to compensate for the temporary loss of income. It would be well worth it in the end.

We lost Pop several months after the purchase, so the Frieseke mural project was tabled while we regained our balance. Some years later, Sonny began work on the three smaller paintings, "Afternoon Tea on the Terrace," "Windy Day at the Beach," and "Mother and Child on the Beach." It took months of focused work to take off the layers of over paint that other hands had applied in their attempted re-interpretation, and get them back as close to their original state as possible. Redwood stretchers had to be ordered as the paintings had never been anywhere but on the walls of the hotel dining room. With snail-like movement and precision, the first painting was finished, the second one followed several months later. They were visually stunning, nothing short of miraculous. "Afternoon Tea on the Terrace" depicted a group of four elegantly dressed women having tea on a terrace as they sat at a white linen covered table with the dark blue sea behind them. Atop the table was a still life of red and pink flowers in a vase, silver teapot, and white cups and saucers with blue trim. "Windy Day at the Beach" was equally impressive. The looming figure of a lady in a long, flowing blue dress in the foreground was being watched by a dapper gent in a white suit and straw hat as he walked in the distant sands, arm in arm with his lady who was dressed in full-length white finery. Striped tents appeared near the water's edge as the salmon sunset sky and dark azure blue sea met in concert.

These were truly two unique American Impressionist works which tipped the hand of what was to come as the other paintings from the mural were to be conserved. We showcased them at the Richmond Museum in the very prestigious organization to which we belonged known as CINOA Exhibition (La Confederation Internationale De Negociants En Oeuvres D'Art) as they were installed opposite one another at the top of the large ascending staircase. We later showed them in an Exhibition called, "A Victorian Era" in Philadelphia at the 23rd Street Armory. We set the stage by constructing a boardwalk on top of the floor accompanied by an arrangement of Victorian wicker love seat, two chairs and a small round table and mounds of salt water taffy of all flavors in the booth. It was a recreation of the essence of Atlantic City with everything except for the smell of fresh roasting peanuts, warm fudge, flashing lights, boardwalk hawkers canvassing their wares, the soothing sounds of summer and the strolling cars. The fans and collectors went wild with nostalgia.

We let the other four large paintings from this mural lay dormant through the 1980s and 1990s as they silently grew in value. Early in 2000, we received a request from the Telfair Museum in Savannah, Georgia to lend two of the four large works, "Under the Striped Umbrella" and "Sunny Afternoon on the Beach" for a year-long tour that involved four museums. After the opening at the Telfair, they would travel to the Dixon Gallery & Gardens in Memphis, and then to the San Diego Museum, and finally to the Terra Museum in Chicago.

Frieseke Afternoon at the Beach

Frieseke Under the Striped Umbrella

We were certainly compliant and excited for the inclusion of these master works in this eye-opening prestigious museum tour. However, they had been rolled up for thirty years and needed to be conserved quickly. We had no idea what state they were in and if they had enough integrity to stand on their own regarding originality. Sonny had died several years prior so finding the right conservator was a major challenge. We had but one shot at getting this right. There could be no mistakes. After careful research and deliberation we elected to go with Barry Bauman of the Chicago Art Conservancy. He had recently been touted in several art journals as the "go to guy" for mural conservation and restoration. We had used him for smaller jobs on occasion in past years and had been very satisfied.

I called him and explained, "Barry we own an important mural from the Shelburne Hotel in Atlantic City. Two of the four large works are going to be included in the upcoming Frieseke Retrospective but they have been rolled up for over thirty years and I have no idea what state they are in now. We faced and removed them properly with professional conservators on site."

"Carl, once we unroll them, you know there's no turning back?" he affirmed emphatically.

"I understand."

"If you want, send all four of them out and we will unroll them and let you know how they look. Understand I cannot even begin to entertain a quote for the work until I see them opened and even then maybe not until I get into them. If that's agreeable, let me know when to expect them."

Our options were limited by the time constraints since the exhibition was only a year away. Even if they were in good and workable condition, we still had to have frames made after conservation completion (in order to know the exact measurements after they were mounted on new stretchers) and then make shipping arrangements from Chicago to our framer in Philadelphia, and then to Savannah for installation and pre-exhibition publicity.

"Okay, I'll have them trucked out to you. Please let me know when they get there safely and call me after you've unrolled them. I'll let you know which two need to be done first."

"Good deal. I'll call you then. Thank you for selecting our firm for the work."

"Our pleasure, we know you'll do this right."

A couple of weeks passed and the paintings were picked up at our gallery in Philadelphia and delivered in Chicago a week later. Barry called to let us know they had arrived safe and sound.

A week later Barry called again to say, "We unrolled them

all and I have to tell you they are in remarkably good condition. Your conservation crew did it right; they are really good. There is a significant amount of over paint that I will need to very carefully remove to get them back to their original state. Then they will need to be relined and in-painted where necessary to fix the various paint losses, and then mounted on redwood stretchers utilizing a very sophisticated spring-loaded stabilizing system."

"Ah, that's great news, Barry. Thank you so much. Go for it, you know our deadlines for the exhibition. We're aware you have to shut out all other work for the year this will take. We will fund you as we agreed."

We got monthly progress reports which softened the blow of the accompanying invoices for services rendered. The exhibition deadlines were met, frames were made, and paintings were delivered on schedule to the Telfair Museum for their debut. Drawing endless crowds, they became a spectacle and an instant classic, literally one of a kind art treasure. From museum to museum, they were winning great acclaim on each leg of the tour. The Shelburne Hotel was razed in 1984 after lying dormant for a decade. The mural was the sole survivor and fortunately it is preserved in history.

We still own these four large treasures and will take our time finding the appropriate home for them—either individually or as a group. Frieseke's star has risen in geometric proportion over the past few decades. At the time we bought the mural from the hotel in Atlantic City, he was considered an important artist but not as highly sought after as works by Childe Hassam, William Merritt Chase, James Abbott McNeil Whistler, John Singer Sargent, and others. Both his popularity and price levels have risen dramatically over the decades. Pop would be all smiles seeing how we handled this phenomenal once-in-a-lifetime acquisition of which he was so proud.

Shawn & Sheri

Brett and Amber

Both Shawn and Brett are now married to wonderful young women, Sheri and Amber respectively, who are very welcome and loving additions to our family. As our business carries forward into the fourth generation, Brett has given the family business a heretofore nonexistent degree of sophistication by bringing us into the electronic age and computerizing our systems. He has also grown into a really good dealer. With a different approach than Shawn's or mine, he has won the hearts and trust of clients.

Chapter Thirty-Two

Fifty-Seven

At fifty-seven years of age, I am ever so quickly moving toward the witching hour. I am constantly reminded of the coming threshold. My father was fifty-eight when he died. That fearful number is looming on the horizon taunting and daring me as I approach. Would I make it to age fifty-eight? Would I surpass it or would my wife be forced to face the future on her own, crippled by the same debilitating wound that my mom endured when her kids became fatherless?

Are we doomed to repeat the past and never break with the grip of tradition? Are we locked into the confines of our destiny? Are we powerless to redesign our paths? Are we programmed to go but so far before the choke collar is tightened, bringing us to a screeching halt? Apparently these are questions only time can answer. We must live on the edge of the precipice unknowing until we have the answer. Then, it will be too late. We are all born to live and die wondering how many days, months, and years we have left. If we live in fear of the ultimate "when," we lose the precious moments as we live them.

"Now" becomes "then" in an instant, and "not yet" becomes "was" whether we consciously experience it or not. Time passes by regardless of whether we enjoy it, fear it, or miss it completely. But, when one has lived through the terrors of loss, a new dimension is opened and refined with trepidation, caution, and reluctance. One becomes a fatalist, resigned to the fact that whatever is going to happen will happen. We can exert our free will and effort, and only hope that we can change what may have been predetermined by a greater force eons ago. We must try; for if we don't, we will surely morph into that very thing we fear. What is there to lose? Nothing—unless we surrender to our fears. Then, we have everything to lose. Then, we become victim to our self-imposed negativity, drawn into the electrically-charged web of fears of our own devices. We must lunge forward with unrelenting willpower and leave denial in our wake.

The mind is a stunningly powerful and complex entity that has the ability to see in multi-faceted ways that we cannot understand on a conscious level. It can simultaneously see what is there, what is not, and what can and cannot be. The mind can arrange, rearrange, create, file, recall, and adapt in a nanosecond on every level of reality and select precisely what it wants us to be, feel, and see. It is a marvelous creation of theater with a cast of characters so vast it is beyond definition. It is an entity so uniquely powerful and insulated it must be revered, awed, respected, and treasured. And, as individually compartmentalized as it is in each of us, it is connected to a much grander network of consciousness to which we all belong. We are all shareholders of an inconceivably larger mechanism that we cannot see, but know exists. Nothing begins or ends, it just transcends and life is but one example of the blueprint into which we have been mapped.

I will not yield to the realistic or unrealistic fears that surface as I near the age of fifty-eight. I will see them as they overwhelm me, analyze them as best I can and move forward. I will feel the fear, relive the tears, and wake up to the breath of fresh air tipped with warm sunlight and that ever so sweet fragrance of life—the ultimate gift to which we have been privileged to receive.

Chapter Thirty-Three

Return to Atlantic Aviation

The sun peeked between puffy gray clouds as temperatures bit sharply with winds flexing their wintry might. Any warmth of the day had long since faded. Shadows loomed with dusk a corner's turn away. We were on our way to the airport to find Atlantic Aviation, a separate entity that private aircraft utilized for business and pleasure without the congestion of the main facility of Philadelphia International.

We had arranged today's meeting to pick up three paintings from a corporate jet when it arrived at 4:15 with our client on board. Schedules were inflexible so this would have to be orchestrated with infallibility. We planned to walk out to the plane and after a brief handshake, take the paintings and head back to the gallery. Our client would be hurriedly whisked away in a waiting limousine for an important board meeting. I was looking forward to seeing our client and the paintings but hadn't counted on the flood of memories that coming here would ensue.

I had spent hours and days at Atlantic Aviation when Pop and I flew together. It was our second home then, and I knew all of the line crews, receptionists, pilots, and airplane owners. It was an informal club for everyone with a passion for flight—a special interest fraternity. The deeply-roasted coffee in the machine cost two bits. It was and exceptional and awakened the senses like a freshly-ground, French-pressed brew. The fumes of exhaust and hot metal from the piston craft were in tandem with the full-throttled takeoffs and smoke-puffed landings that occurred in continuous cycles. Ash trays were filled with charred cinders and tan butts.

My memories of the place had faded, and after thirty-four years, I was unsure of its whereabouts. After a couple of wrong turns, we saw Atlantic Aviation a quarter of a mile ahead. We passed several inactive hangars and facilities—vestiges of past generations, rusting away under the pale and faded sky blue. As we turned into the drive, we circled and pulled to the front entranceway double doors. Nothing looked familiar.

Shawn and I went into the building and walked up to the reception desk as the girl greeted us, "Hi, can I help you?"

"Yes, we're here to meet a client coming in from Wyoming at 4:15." I gave her the call letters of the jet.

"They're about ten minutes out. I will let you know when they are on the ground."

"Thank you."

We walked around looking out the large glass windows. All of the piston aircraft I had known so well had been replaced by multi-million-dollar jets of varying sizes and ages. It was a new day.

"They're down, sir. They should be here in a minute or so."

"Good. It is okay if we wait outside until they get here?"

"Sure."

The large Falcon jet pulled up and we got the nod of approval to approach the plane. The twin jet engines were whining down as the forward steps opened and our client deplaned and headed toward us. We shook hands and enjoyed a few sentences of rushed conversation. The paintings were brought to us in their boxes by the porter. We waved thanks to our client who turned to get into a waiting limousine. We loaded the paintings into the Suburban, exited the area, and headed back to the gallery.

As we left Atlantic Aviation, a torrent of emotions overcame me. I stepped back thirty-four years into the vacuous textbook of history that could only be accessed by vicarious remembrance. The files, though unlocked, were limited in their retrieval. Cobwebs clouded my vision with the sad realization that there was no possible entry back through the closed door to that wonderful era.

A few weeks later I got another call to meet our client at the airport to pick up more paintings. Confident I had relived the past, this trip would be easier. This time I would drive solo to Atlantic Aviation.

I arrived fifteen minutes ahead of schedule, walked into the building, and identified myself, "I'm Carl David, checking on the arrival of my client's jet."

"Due in any minute," informed the receptionist.

"I used to fly out of here thirty-four years ago. It looks so different now."

"Oh, you must mean the old building." She pointed to her right. "We moved about ten years ago; that's why you don't recognize it."

It suddenly made sense.

I walked out to meet the client, glancing over at the old facility. Empty and standing alone, she looked lonely as if awaiting the days of the past to return and revive her—to give her life again and restore her purpose. She'll undoubtedly keep waiting and hoping until she realizes that her old friends won't be coming back.

"Hello, Captain!" I'd done a lot of business with this particular client over the years and we'd grown to be friends.

"Carl, good to see you again." When he put his arm around me, it seemed like Pop had just landed and was with me—difficult to explain, but very comforting.

"I have the paintings for you."

"I'm sure they are wonderful."

"I can't stay and talk now, but we'll talk in a day or so."

"I understand. I look forward to hearing from you."

I took the paintings, shook the Captain's hand and we went our separate ways.

I drove away remembering all of the love and goodness that had been bestowed upon me. My face was wet with sweet tears as I counted myself so fortunate. I was strangely fulfilled.

Those two visits to Atlantic Aviation were a blessing. We got some great inventory and I got to voyage into the recesses of time where nothing changes, where everything is good—a place to soothe the soul, be reassured, and consoled.

Chapter Thirty-four
Return to Bader Field

After visiting Atlantic Aviation, I thought it was time to pay a visit to another old friend—Bader Field. I might as well get it all out of my craw while the airfield was still there. I needed to return to what I consider hallowed ground as this old airfield was the very last place I felt my father's embrace as we hugged tightly before he got back into the Aztec to fly home in 1973. I never suspected or even anticipated the emotional ambush that was just around the corner. The horror of that 3:50 a.m. telephone call from Mom would become a perpetual living nightmare of decimating proportion. The suturing of that wound had taken decades. Although the profuse bleeding had stopped, the dressings continually required changing as the weeping of the wound ebbed and waned, never quite healing to completion. His final words that day, "I Love You" forever permeate my soul.

The first known usage of the term "air-port" appeared in a

newspaper article in 1919, in reference to Bader Field. Bader Field opened in 1910 and was authorized to provide passenger service in 1911 and continued until the 1980s. However, by the 1990s, activity at Bader Field declined significantly in favor of Atlantic City International, which was located approximately nine miles northwest. When the casinos opened in 1976, the Atlantic City International was deemed financially necessary. Gamblers and high rollers alike could fly in on their own private jets to try their luck. It was all part of the overall plan to bring larger revenues into the dying Atlantic City and secure the future of the Grand Old Dame.

At four o'clock, the sun was still baking and the sultry July breezes were of little consolation. I headed through the old Atlantic City Circle and illegally veered right after missing the turning lane. Ahead on the right, just past the overpass was the stadium constructed adjacent to the old Bader airfield. The actual runways and taxiway are still there for the moment. However, there is a major casino development deal in the works, and when finalized will once and for all wipe away the remaining vestiges of the Bader Field.

Bader Field Mold Short

I was summoned inexplicably with a compulsion that drew me

like the relentless gravity of a black hole. I turned in at the light and drove up the paved street, passing with irreverence the sign that read "Parking $10." I had no intention of parking. I simply begged a view into the window of days gone by.

Feeling the whooshing of blood in my head as my pulse quickened with apprehension, I drove fifty yards further to the decaying cyclone fence at the far rear of the grounds. There sat dormant the remnants of the old airway as the oil-stained asphalt still bore some of the yellow painted lines curving toward what was once the little food shack and Unicom. I pulled up out of sight of the street traffic, turned off the motor and sat. I was stilled by the wilderness that snuffed out this place. It had once been so vibrant and lively.

Bader Taxiway & Unicom

I got out of the car with an ambivalent mix of fear and anxiety and peered through the small wire rims of the rusted fence. The old runway looked like a child who'd been orphaned without regard. The silence was jarring but for the renewed screaming playback of turbulent history in my head. Everything rushed back in an instant. I was no longer fifty-eight. I was once again twenty-four years old. Beads of sweat dotted my head and as I felt my body retreat into that horrific timeless warp. I took some long, deep breaths and mustered as much composure as I could.

I needed to get to a better vantage point to see and feel what had been there years ago. I pushed the door open. The rust-laden squeal drew no attention. I walked out to the center of what I remembered to be the runway, knelt down, and began capturing mental images of what once was. I sat down on the hot strip sharing her loneliness and waited with longing for the impossible return of the Aztec. I imagined those dual props sputtering to a halt, Mom and Pop getting out of the red and white bird. I felt the hugs of yesterday.

Bader Field Runway

I stood up and looked around feeling an upwelling sadness. I felt bad for the place but worse for myself. We'd both suffered an irreversible loss. We'd met here so many times, and enjoyed each other's company. The feeling of richness and fulfillment was always there. The simple food, the airport coffee, the myriad of personalities, the airplanes, the sounds of the propellers slicing through the humidity, the squeal of the tires as they kissed the runway, the prop wash that rippled my shirt as the planes turned away to taxi. It was now so painfully vacant.

The old metal communication shack was a lone memorial still standing. There it lay speechless amidst the weeds. I wanted to leave but couldn't. I wanted to stay but had no more words. Heavy with sadness, I got back into the car and turned back to Route 40. The crunching of the pebbles beneath the tires was a friendly companion as a cloud of dust trailed behind. At the exit light, I mistakenly turned right and slowly headed toward the roadway when I noticed another dirt road to my right. It appeared to go nowhere, dead-ending with another cyclone fence that overlooked an empty bone yard with old rusting piles of metals. I took the turn. The unpaved pathway, littered with debris, veered left and continued on invisibly into a bend. I followed the path for several hundred feet driving over weeds, rocks, and incidental bits of trash. I took one final twist to the right. I was stunned with delight at what I saw. It was the actual runway on which we used to land. It was invisible from the outside and was overrun by foot-high weeds, which had pushed their way up through the black asphalt like unopposed soldiers. What I had mistakenly thought to be the runway almost an hour before was actually the taxiway.

It all became perfectly clear as the pieces began to fit nicely into the recesses of my mind. The memories had been shrouded by years of self-imposed amnesia. I got out of the car feeling as though I'd just uncovered a vein of gold after so many decades of searching. I crunched over the bed of weeds and found myself standing at the end of the runway. I reveled in awe as the length of the old landing strip lay before me. The sparkle of Pop's brilliant blue eyes, his overflowing warmth, his kindness, his larger-than-life presence, but especially his unconditional love filled me with the will to go on and know that it will be all right.

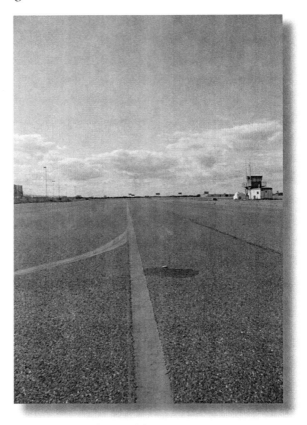

Bader Field Taxiway

I began taking photographs of the place I'd so treasured all those years ago until it kicked me senseless, assaulting me with the death of my father. I was at long last able to come back as the prodigal son who had wandered off. I was then able to face what had petrified me for so many years. It was no longer so deeply painful, only mournful. Being there provided a newfound level of comfort.

The tears of sadness that streaked my face had ingredients of relief within them. I'd ventured a long way and the journey was finally at its end. I breathed deeply and stared aimlessly at the barren asphalt strip before me and ingested the hot afternoon breezes as history repeated itself in my very being.

I slowly turned and reluctantly walked back to the car, stopping and glancing over my shoulder every few yards for just a bit more sweetness to store in the vault of my unconscious. I hopped onto the running boards of my waiting car to capture a few more images. One thing was certain; at some point in the future this place would never look the same.

And so, I'd come full circle. Summoned to Bader Field in these early days of July of 2007, I have been allowed as much closure as anyone can actually achieve. This is where it all began and this is where it has now ended. "See ya Pop, I love you."

Chapter Thirty-Five

Horrible Date in Infamy

It is now forty-two years after the fact and today is a horrid reminder of the violent loss we all suffered so long ago when we lost Bruce. I always know that the time of year is approaching as summer ends and fall replaces it with that crisp, cool air tainted with the foreboding date, October thirteenth. I always think I'll get through it with blind ignorance because so much time has passed. I fail to acknowledge that no matter the distance in years, the scar of that event is permanent. There is no walking away, no forgetting—only avoidance—then the unrelenting forces of the universe remind me. No matter how much effort is expended to erase it, no matter how much I redirect the emotions toward suppression, no matter what the mode of distraction, the emotional body will win. The symptoms of gut ache, headache, nightmares, fatigue, indifference, agitation, anger, rage, inability to focus, flawed judgment, impaired decision making, short temper, irritability, and general malaise will persist and not relinquish their grip until the deeply buried pain is allowed to surface. Some things in life are programmed with permanence and we must work with them, not futilely against them.

So, as this day approached this year, I maintained a leveled calm with an occasional episode of agitation but overall nothing unusual. The stiff neck and headache appeared in tandem on a mild scale as I felt the grip of the past sneaking up on me. As I worked through the day at the gallery, the headache subsided with an inordinate quenching of coffee establishing a temporary victory. And so the eleventh came and went with relative ease. The twelfth redoubled its strength and gifted me with a persistent headache. Coffee after coffee, no change; the pounding persisted like the stranger's unrelenting knocking on the door. I yawned to release some of the pressure over my eyes. A few drops of moisture ebbed, but no difference as the suffering continued.

I called Alan in California. "Hey, are you okay? It's the anniversary week of Bruce's death."

"I was not aware of the date, but I have been feeling weird all day. You know, I've never really been quite certain whether it was the thirteenth or fourteenth."

"It was sometime during the night of the thirteenth, but Pop found him on the morning of the fourteenth, so it was actually either or both."

"How are you doing?"

"I'm okay..." My words cracked with vibrato, my eyes wetted quickly. "My body bears witness with symptoms similar to those he might have experienced as he took his last breath—headache and neck pain."

Alan's tender concern hurled me back to the day he was standing at the bottom of the steps of our house on Cliveden Street in Mount Airy. He had the dreaded job of telling me Bruce was dead as I walked panic stricken through that front door. His words blackened my world in an instant. I left my body, thrust into a vacuous place that for the rest of my life would remain a realm of contentious objection. That blade of steel cut so deeply, I didn't care if I survived the wound. Bruce's suicide was a senseless act that defies explanation and logic. There were no answers, nor would there ever be. The mystery would remain unsolved.

Shortly after my call to Alan, the phone rang.

"Alan just called me to make sure I was okay," Mom explained. "He told me you called to check on him and that he was very touched by it. This was the first time he ever called me on this day and I felt quite moved as well."

"It was a difficult day then, and it still is now."

"I'll never forget the look of horror on your face when you and Alan were slumped in each other's arms at the bottom of the stairs after he delivered that terrible message." She started to weep.

That did it. The rest of my tears rose in a rushing tide as we relived those dreadful moments.

I have fifty-nine years now, but somewhere in the recesses of my life I am and will forever be sixteen years old. The nightmare resides but somehow we simply have to live with it, acknowledge it, and deal with the feelings as they arise and surface. The search for answers, clues, anything at all to grasp has been ongoing for forty-two years now. The torment rages on with reminders as people from the past appear from time to time. It was rumored that Bruce questioned his professor about suicide in his class that fateful night at Temple University. Someone else later confessed they knew something but were sworn to secrecy and would never divulge the information, not even to us. And so, there were clues here and there but nothing more than vague references leading to further abstraction. Did it really matter? Bruce is gone; his bright blue eyes closed forever and locked in darkness, his handsome, rugged body below ground never to be seen again. His love and sensitivity and wry sense of humor are now just a memory. Our lives are clouded by the gaping vacancy of our beloved brother, son, and best friend.

Chapter Thirty-Six

You Can't Go Far

Half way through March in 2008, Mom was involuntarily designated, "Last Woman Standing." Her only remaining sister, Eve, passed but hours after we went to see her in the hospital. There would be a graveside service the next day at Roosevelt Memorial Park, a place with which we were all too familiar. I was asked to say a few words. I agreed to try, if I could get them out.

With very little sleep, we embarked the next day to the cemetery around noon leaving sufficient time to work around any traffic we might encounter. Our family and friends gathered in sadness at the passing of this kind, gentle, and ever so giving lady. The rabbi spoke with a tribute befitting of this tender soul, lauding her praises and even interjecting some humor to temper the weight of the loss. Closing prayers ensued and in orthodox fashion, the plain wooden box in which she had been enshrouded was lowered. Shovels full of dirt were cast upon it by all who wanted to partake, symbolizing a mitzvah as it was explained.

While we were there, we decided to visit Bruce and Pop's graves. It took a bit of searching to find the row where they were buried as we were a bit disoriented. It was Arlyn who remembered definitively that it was the section that faced the mausoleum. I parked the car, got out, and walked the marker-littered path to the bend in front of the shrubs that bordered the section. When I saw Bruce's marker and Pop's next to it, my eyes overflowed with sorrow. I motioned to the others that I had found them.

Mom stood over Bruce's grave and sobbed, "How could you do this to us?"

I cried like it was yesterday as I stood behind her with my hands on her shoulders. I tried to be as silent as I could, not to upset her even more. We moved to Pop's grave and stood there sobbing as if time had ceased to exist. It was 1965 and 1973 and 2008 all at once with no discernible delineation; no difference at all. The horror flooded in an instant with an irrevocable permanence. Time was unforgiving, nothing changed; our resilience would get us to the next time but it was like the movie *Groundhog Day*. There was simply no escaping it.

Arlyn's refrain always echoes within me, "You never get over it; you just learn to live with it."

It doesn't matter how far away you get from it, it is always with you; you can't go far. But in reality you can't have the good without the bad. The Universe demands balance and will make sure it exists, regardless. If we didn't have the loving goodness and richness of our loved ones, then we wouldn't have the pain and conversely if we didn't have the pain, then we would not have had the love in the first place.

Chapter Thirty-Seven

The Everlasting Fear

⤜⤏ ⤍⤏

If there's one thing life has taught me, it's that nothing lasts forever—whether it's good or bad. The memories of my days with Pop are locked into my cells so securely that I can borrow them as many times as I like and then return them for safe-keeping. It's as if they're timeless; there for the asking and virtually indestructible. I can relive so many of the wondrous experiences at a moment's whim and reconstruct them as if I were viewing the same motion picture over and over again. I can narrow in on certain episodes, facial expressions, and even auditory sensations. The most awesome characteristic is the sense of reality these things conjure up; so much so that even fifteen or twenty or thirty years later when certain memory cells are tickled and exposed, emotions are triggered unconsciously. Tears will come to the forefront, muscles will tighten, or perhaps spontaneous laughter will erupt. It is as though time has reversed itself and yesterday has arrived in full fashion again; a zone of twilight with no beginning and no end—just continual linkage of the generations.

But through all the scars and wounds sustained, I've been hit with a numbing question which goes unanswered. It's an abstraction with no guarantee and no promise, only a lease of indeterminable length! Am I next? When? Will I be struck down with a major coronary before my time too? Am I under too much stress? Have I consumed too many and too much of the wrong foods? Are the check-ups accurate or have the doctors missed something? Will I make it to see sixty years and beyond or will I be snuffed out like a dying candle? Those questions haunt me because of the God-awful shock which befell me in my early twenties. In the long run, it's made me take a good hard look at myself and take note of my vulnerability as a human being and realize my limitations as a mortal. It has made me hunger for more time with my wife and children, and pray against all odds that I do in fact have many more years in the works. I don't want them to undergo the wrenching cheat, pain, and separation of such a loss.

My life has been full, and though I'm only in my late fifties, I have done, seen, and participated in life's finest and richest offerings. My family is still tender and young and I want for them all of the happiness and ease of living that can be arranged. I have committed myself to the notion of staying healthy and providing them with all of the splendor which was showered upon me through those phenomenal years when Pop was ever so much in my life. I didn't wage an epic battle of emotions after being run through with the sword of my father's death, to just give up and relinquish the spoils of the reconstruction of my life! I have worked plenty hard to get where I am now. Nothing was handed to me; what was given was never without commensurate responsibility, so consequently becoming spoiled was not an issue. The fear of losing it all follows me like a shadow. It's like a time bomb hidden beyond my vision lurking somewhere in the recesses of time.

In recent years, I have exercised a serious degree of caution with food intake, trying to avoid being felled by an army of trigger-happy saturated fats that long to narrow crucial arterial passages. Sedentary has never been my style. I'm too easily bored to simply lay around and disintegrate. I don't smoke and I'm very active; however, I refuse to get nuts about rigid regimented exercise. So, the only death-like characteristic left is stress. Well, I can't say we're strangers; we've met too often, but I think I'm pretty good at negotiating it. I own an intense kind of personality. I do everything with total commitment; I feel with every ounce of emotion. My parents used to call me "sensitive" to which I took great offense when I was young, as if it were a sign of weakness in my character. To the contrary, I was too sensitive then to understand. Today, I totally agree that I'm deeply sensitive, but I now appreciate the aptness of the label. I laugh hard—sometimes convulsively—and I cry genuine tears at sadness. Quite an achievement for a guy who grew up in an era when "men" didn't cry! That was acceptable only for girls and women—others were viewed as a sniveling wimp! Can you imagine what happens when you deny vent to such a powerful relief valve? Well, if you are truly a sensitive being, certain circumstances, thoughts, and remembrances will open the flood gate of emotion. I anger when I'm mistreated, and I respond with vitriolic force. I love with discrimination, deeply, and with total devotion and absolute unrestraint. When I fall, I fall hard. When I play, I play hard. Total immersion is my way, and it supports my philosophy of "Do it right, or don't do it at all."

I try to get a handle on stress by acting with an appropriate response. Whichever emotion springs up first, wins. I enjoy analyzing situations and problems—first on an intellectual level, but more introspectively on a gut level. By understanding what I'm feeling and which emotional forces are anchoring me, I know the appropriately action to take. One of the key words is "relax" not to the point of numbness, but just enough to appraise the situation clearly and to deal with it from a different posture. Most crises are workable given a novel approach, a little time, and the ability to compromise a bit. Mediation is crucial and what one must do is loosen up the demands and be satisfied to meet in the middle. Business stress is tough, but workable if you're willing to exercise a little patience. Stress of a personal nature is another story. I believe it's human nature to worry but fortunately ninety-right percent of worry is anticipation and doesn't ever come to pass. The other two percent is horrible and has to be fought with all conceivable defense.

Nonetheless, I wonder: Have I handled things well enough to survive in the long run? Have I taken too many hits from stress? Is it too late? Did I ingest too much junk food in college? All that fried chicken I devoured, and countless dozens of ice cold 12-ounce cans of soda! Ah, those incredible bubbles and how they burnt on the way down my throat. The slivers of sweetened ice that floated atop the semi frozen liquid! How satisfying it was then. A habit I quit at the conclusion of college in 1970. Maybe ingesting huge and varied epicurean treats was the way in which I dealt with stress in those days. Since then I've grown sensible regarding dietary habits, and now hope that I didn't do too much damage to the old system.

≈ ≈

Chapter Thirty-Eight

Age Fifty-Nine

≈ ≈

Having successfully traversed the uncertain sands of my fifty-eighth year without demise, a new border was staring at me with unprecedented challenge. My fifty-ninth birthday was just days away and I was devoid of interest in it. It seemed incongruous, foreign, and inappropriate. I felt no excitement or victory in having passed the symbolic wall representing age fifty-eight.

Arlyn, Shawn and Sheri, and Brett and Amber were all in a festive mood, eagerly looking to mark the occasion with joy. "What do you want to do to celebrate? Where do you want to go for dinner?"

"Oh, something simple and not expensive just as long as we are all together." I really meant it, what better way to mark an occasion.

Late in the evening of January 29, Arlyn and I were about to doze off when she reminded me, "It will be your birthday in the breath of another hour."

"Yep," was all I could muster.

After a fitful and restless night's sleep, I arose the next morning to find Arlyn downstairs having coffee. She had been up for an hour. "Happy Birthday!" she smiled and gave me a loving embrace.

"Thanks Babe." I had forgotten it was my birthday. It felt to me like any other day; it was nothing special.

Later at work, while I was enjoying putting deals together, people called with greetings of congratulations. Everyone wanted to know how I was going to celebrate. My answer was the same, "I'm just going to enjoy the day." That was truly how I felt; I was happy to have family and friends in my life. They are the real gifts.

When Brett and I were alone he said, "Hey Pop, I bet it feels good to have made it past fifty-eight." He was well aware of the difficulty I'd had about making it to the age my father was when he died. That brief snippet of a statement strongly wedged itself deeply into my subconscious and then went blank.

I nodded in acknowledgment. "Yep, it does." My eyed welled with tears.

After a really nice day at work, I went home, longing for Arlyn's hugs and kisses. Her smile always pierced the veil of any armor I wore and melted away the layers of emotional defense. As I came through the front door, I knelt down to pet Nellie who was waiting eagerly for my arrival at the foot of the stairs. She is such a sweet soul who always makes me feel good. Arlyn swept across the kitchen proudly holding up the magnificent chocolate cake.

"Look what I made for you!" It had been a long time since anyone baked a cake for me. I was so touched.

"What a delicious gesture of love! You made my day." I hugged her tightly, never wanting to let go. Something deep inside me began to thaw. "Thank you so much. It feels incredible to be loved so much. What a sweet thing to do." I was finally allowing the light of the day to enter and warm me. My resistance was weakening.

Arlyn and Carl David 2008

A day later while at the gallery, I was working on the computer when a sudden wave of dizziness overcame me. I panicked when I couldn't stop the spinning. This was an emotional reaction to something. I know myself well enough to know that when I have repressed emotions because they always surface of their own volition; sometimes violently. I know this had to do with Pop and feelings I had but briefly given vent to before locking them down in a seemingly impenetrable safe.

I calmed myself as best I could and acknowledged a trickle of few tears. The release helped but not completely. Settled a bit, I drove home looking for music on the radio which would help me to get in touch with my feelings. Twenty minutes later I was home and told Arlyn of my episode. For several days, I had been thinking about the theme from *Exodus*, so I went to the computer looking for a sound rendition of it. It had been years since I had heard it. It was such a beautiful and powerfully emotive melody. After hearing a couple of versions, my head began spinning again. I called Arlyn to come to me.

"Don't you know why that made you dizzy?" she stated. "Your father used to play that."

"We used to play it together." I started to cry. "The pain of loss is still so damned strong. Even after all these years, the scar still opens and closes like the gills of a shark. At times, it is dormant but the mere flicker of a memory ignites it with a fury and it attacks with a vengeance. I wish the pain would just go away once and for all."

"It doesn't and it won't. You can only learn to live with it." She hugged me as I allowed the sadness to pass. The anxiety quelled and I became calmer and more balanced.

A couple of nights later we were walking through the mall hoping to find a few things we needed before the big Palm Beach Jewelry, Art & Antiques Show in which we were exhibiting again this year.

"I really don't feel fifty-nine," I confided. "I still feet fifty-eight." It was an odd number that didn't quite fit.

"You're just one day older; that's all." She smiled.

When I told her what Brett had said a few days earlier, she raised her eyebrows with pride for her son's astute perception, "You have survivor's guilt don't you?"

I choked, stunned by her assessment. I nodded, wiped my eyes and admitted, "I absolutely do. I have lived longer than my father. I'm older now than he was when he died. It's very odd to outlive one's own father at such a young age. He was far too young; his death far too premature."

On a brighter note, Mom just had her ninetieth birthday. We celebrated with her friends and all of our family. We took over a private room on the second floor of Le Bec Fin, a fabulous and legendary French restaurant in Center City, Philadelphia.

An epicurean delight, to say the least. George Perrier, chef-owner extraordinaire, has been a very good friend of our family for thirty-five years or longer. The room was pure French elegance, the food divine and everyone had a warm loving time. It was akin to being in Versailles with candle lit tables and traditional but not stuffy French service.

Flora Celebrating her 90th Birthday

Beyond everything was Mom in her glory. To look at her one would never believe she was older than her mid-sixties. She is a beautiful woman, through and through. And to think that we were worried that she might not survive Pop's death.

About the Author: Carl David

Born in Philadelphia, Carl David is the third descendant of a four-generation art dealer family specializing in American and European nineteenth- and twentieth-century paintings, watercolors, and drawings.

Carl earned a Bachelor of Arts with a degree in business in 1970 from Oglethorpe College in Atlanta, Georgia. *Bader Field* is his second published book. He is also the author of *Collecting and Care of Fine Art* published by Crown Publishers (1981). His article "Martha Walter" appeared in the May 1978 issue of *American Art Review*.

Mr. David was a charter member of Sotheby's.com (New York), and is a member of the Art and Antique Dealers League, and La Confederation Internationale De Negotiants En Oeuvres D'Art.

He has served as judge for the Manayunk Art Show, co-chaired the gallery committee of Rittenhouse Row, guest auctioneer for WHYY, and panel member for the Art News World Art Market (New York). Carl has been involved with The Friends of Rittenhouse Square, The Free Appraisal Clinic, The Philadelphia Art Museum, The Dealer's Committee for US Artists, and Rittenhouse Row.

Using his knowledge of the fine arts, Carl has taught "Collecting Fine Art" at Main Line School Night, and served as a guest lecturer at the Philadelphia Library, the Pennsylvania Academy of the Fine Arts, and the U.S. Artists Exhibition (2004–2006). As a philanthropist, David has used art as a backdrop to organize and produce fundraising exhibitions for the Washington, D.C. branch of the National Center For Missing & Exploited Children, the Delaware Valley Burn Foundation, the American Red Cross and the Make a Wish Foundation.

Carl has given appraisals and consultations for: the Brandywine River Museum, American Bar Association, The White House, Office of the Attorney General, State of New York, FBI, State Department, Philadelphia Museum of Art, Pennsylvania Academy of the Fine Arts, Union League Club of Philadelphia, Buck Hill Falls Art Association, Law Firm of Ronald A. White, Law Firm of Morgan, Lewis & Bockius, the DuPont Family, the Wilmington Library, The Hagley Museum, Strassburger, McKenna, Gutnick & Potter (Pittsburgh), Wilkes College (Sordoni Art Gallery) Wilkes Barre, PA, University of Virginia, Cigna, and Sun Oil Company.

Along with his interest and career as an art dealer, Carl has serious involvement in both music and photography. He does all of the gallery photography work and has photographic images hosted on Webshots.com and istockphoto.com. He has written several ballads. His first ("My Love For You") was professionally mastered, arranged, and produced by Dave Appell of Decca Records and Cameo-Parkway Records.

For many years, Carl David has had a serious interest in and has been a proponent of all aspects of healing. He has woven spirituality and energy work into his daily life. As a firm believer in "paying it forward," he knows that karmic debts must be paid, and is very cognizant of keeping a clear conscious and doing the right thing. Life has thrown him some nasty turns, but instead of being bitter and resentful, he has tried to learn from each experience and shift his focus toward something positive.

Breinigsville, PA USA
04 April 2010
235475BV00005B/17/P